Autnenuc

Jason Moore

Discovering the Life You were Built to Live

Dedication:

To my wife Sarah, the original Flame Keeper.

TABLE OF CONTENTS

Part I:

COMATOSE

Chapter 1
The Lost Children

"Honesty is the first chapter in the book of wisdom."
-Thomas Jefferson

How did we get here as a people? We strive for more and more and more but can't seem to remember what we started working for all that time ago. We have lost our way. A general malaise has descended on our country. We look around to see dual income families who still can't make ends meet. We have children being pushed to ever more heights in sports and academics yet suffering from unprecedented levels of anxiety and depression. We find "reality" TV has taken over for actual reality living.

More and more people are marching like zombies to jobs every day that strip away their desire for a better tomorrow. Every piece of advice young people receive is focused on achieving financial success for the sole purpose of satisfying the consumerism demand of society. The entire education system of our nation is designed to push young adults into careers that appear successful, regardless of whether it benefits them or society.

We have reached a place where adults are literally defined by their occupation. Never is a thought given to whether these careers provide a satisfaction that feeds our internal need to matter. The sobering truth of this new paradigm is most people simply don't remember what it is to matter. The raging fires that forged our nation and pushed generations to amazing accomplishments have simply died away to ashes. Lost in fear, division, and complacency. Our dreams have given way to a machine designed to produce more efficient, less individualized members of society.

Yet through it all, there remains inside every person an ember of the passion to once again find true calling, ignite the fire, and leave a mark on this world.

The good news is there are a few who refuse to go quietly. The few who desire to pour fuel on the fire and watch it burn. There is a growing movement of people who insist on finding a better path forward and blazing it for all those around. These people are committed to living the AUTHENTIC life they were intended to live. They are the Flame Keepers, and this book is dedicated to them.

Chapter 2
A HERO Rises

"We know what we are but know not what we may be."
-William Shakespeare

E very hero needs a back story. We yearn to know where the internal strength comes from. How did this person develop the courage to step out and become a hero? What choices were made to bring us to the current moment of triumph?

I genuinely wish I could give you a hero's back story, but sadly I am no hero. I am a flawed, and in some ways, broken man. I have made more mistakes than any person has the right to in this life. Yet, I recognize the opportunity to change the narrative. I WANT to be the hero of someone's story. That's why I feel it's important to lay out my story and provide a glimpse of all the broken pieces. I want to show every person I meet that the hero you are looking for is already inside, if you are only willing to put on the cape.

I was raised in what by most standards would be a charmed household. My mom and dad were middle class with a hint of wealth that provided me every advantage growing up. I attended great schools, participated in any sport I enjoyed, and was surrounded by a solid loving family at home. My siblings were a good deal younger, which brought me independence and freedom as I grew since my parents needed to move on to assisting them. In summary, I had it good. It all sounds amazing, except there is another side of the story.

My dad is actually my stepdad. No less my dad for it as he made me the man I am in every way. However, my biological father was a heavy influence in my life as well. He showed me what alcoholism and destruction look like. He served as a reminder of what failing to gain an education would mean for me. He also left a hole in me as he moved onto his new family and treated me as optional. The resentment tore at me for years. It also meant I was raised by a mother who was intent on me being NOTHING like my father. This is where the story really begins.

I was a brash and arrogant child (I am trying to change this as an adult), but one who truly wanted to please my parents. I was a straight "A" student who rarely caused trouble in school. I found success in most things I attempted. I was near the top of my class in high school and was accepted to an elite university on scholarship. The problem? I had no idea who or what I was. No idea where I wanted to go in life. My mother's family was and still are titans of business. There was never a day in my life I didn't feel pressure to be like them. To succeed like them. Every day growing up I was held to a standard I could never reach. It truly felt like no one was ever proud of me.

I certainly can't speak to what people truly felt, but I struggled to live up to the dream plan laid out for me. My outward appearance was one of an all-American middle-class kid. I learned to play the part expected of me simply as a way of keeping others off my back. I resented it with all I was. It caused me to lash out many times over the years. I never truly went off the deep end, but I did create self-destructive habits.

Fast forward to graduating, getting married, having kids and enjoying strong professional results. Still it never mattered. My family remained displeased or disappointed with me for some reason or another. I spent a solid 10 years living the dreams of someone else. All the while my depression grew, and my life crumbled from within. I bounced around and slid further into jobs I hated, trying to prove I was a success. Eventually the bottom fell out. My first marriage failed. My health took a severe turn for the worse. My career cracked and broke. My finances imploded. I was staring down the barrel of complete meltdown of everything I thought mattered to me. I eventually considered suicide. Luckily my children mean entirely too much to me for that to ever be a real consideration. However, my desperation was growing. Something had to give.

September 21, 2010 the tide turned. Sarah walked through the front door of my condo and into my life. From the first day I knew her she thought I was a hero. I sadly knew the truth was anything but that. However, I was going to give all I had to making her believe it. She breathed a new life into me, and I began fighting back against years of frustration and resentment at being told, against all facts, I was a failure. I would prove to the world that I was not beaten. I was not broken. I was finally Awake and Alive. This girl would be the reason I got off the mat and started rebuilding.

The final flash point happened on a quiet day at lunch while sitting on a bench beside a pond. I was waiting to return to a job so stressful it was literally killing me and draining away my soul. As I sat dreading a return to the office, an older gentleman approached, and we struck up a conversation. He asked what I did for a living. I explained to him I was a controller for a very large real estate firm. He asked if I made good money and I said yes. He asked if I was well regarded and I said yes. He then asked if I was happy and I said absolutely NOT. I emphasized I was miserable. He asked a question I will never forget, "Why do you go?". I was floored because I had no answer. At all. I could not give one solid, rationale answer as to why I continued to waste my life in that job. Money perhaps, but that is a sorry excuse for a reason. An "impressive" title. No, that meant nothing to me. I simply could not answer him. This was a place I spent upwards of 70 hours a week (I mentioned this place sucked right?), and I could not find one reason to justify why I tolerated the misery. This struck me as absurd.

I returned to my office, typed up a resignation letter, and placed it on my boss' desk. He asked me where I was going. I said, "I have no idea, but I am not coming here anymore."

When I got home, I told Sarah what happened. The next moment changed my life forever. She said it was ok. That simple. That powerful. No judgement. No condemnation. Just support. Sarah told me she believed I could do anything, and I should just go "be me". No more pleasing others. No more chasing other's dreams. Just go be the best version of Jason. In that exact moment, the spark was ignited, and the flame roared to life. From that moment forward I decided to dedicate my life to changing the story for everyone I come in contact with.

I now teach college classes on personal finance, work for an amazing company that improves educational opportunities for disadvantaged youth, give speeches about life passion and purpose to groups all over, and smile every damn day of it. I have no idea if my family is proud of me anymore, but it also doesn't matter because I am. This is why every person I help in this life and every story that is rewritten for those I meet is a testament to Sarah's belief in me. In the end, I guess this was the origin story for a hero. It's just that the hero is my wife Sarah, as she is the original Flame Keeper.

Chapter 3
THE RESISTANCE Begins

"Believe you can, and you are halfway there"
-Theodore Roosevelt

As Authentic has grown and been presented over time, I have been honored to receive many incredible stories from people who made the decision to follow this path and found incredible results. These stories mean more than any pay I could ever receive for the work. To hear from people all over of their life changing based on simple decisions I helped them make is too incredible for words. Every person I help is recompense for anyone I have hurt and repayment to all those that supported me. The following is my absolute favorite story from this journey and hopefully will provide insight into how far your dreams can take you if you are willing to trust yourself.

A HORSE-RIDING SUPERHERO IS BORN

The second time I ever stood in front of a crowd and presented this material was to a group of finance majors. All the smiling faces in front of me were hungry to hear how a career in finance would unfold and bring them the riches of the world. I was presenting on careers in finance so the assumption was I would speak about being a controller, finance manager, stockbroker, insurance agent, financial planner, or something of the like. I had a completely different approach in mind.

My first question pulled the rug out from under the students. I asked how they viewed the local high school they graduated from. Clearly confused, they were not sure how to answer. I continued down the path. What are all the things a school actually handles on a daily basis? Students sure. Education, of course. Let's try going deeper. How about being the largest employer in most towns? How about having the largest buildings in many places? Throw in transportation, hiring, firing, food service, sports programs, facility maintenance, and technology services. I asked them what it sounded like when I listed things in that way. A brave young lady finally answered, "a business". Bingo. Schools are a huge business and deserve to be supported by people who understand the concepts of business. That's my job in a nutshell. I use my financial skills to help schools run like a business and be more financially stable. In turn, changing the lives of thousands of young people.

I continued with this same young lady and asked her what she was truly passionate about. (Side note, I can't go more than about 3 minutes into any conversation with a new person without asking this question.) She immediately sat up straighter, and excitedly said equestrian jumping.

This young lady loved to compete in horse jumping. She followed quickly with a version of, "but you can't make a living doing that". I fired back. I asked if she had been to a certain horse stable near the university that was famous for hosting large competitions. She of course had been there. She loved the place and went into detail of some of the times she had competed there.

In the ultimate twist of irony, years earlier I had interviewed at these stables to be the business manager. I didn't know horses or barns well enough to get the job. This girl did though. Her mind was blown. It had never occurred to her that someone actually has to run the business of a horse stable.

I went on to spend the next 45 minutes or so explaining to these students that your dream job is not in a title. It is not in the same job everyone who has come before you dreamed of. It's unique to you as an individual. To really find a path for your life where you will love waking up every day requires you to combine all the aspects of who you are with the skills you acquire. It was a well-received presentation, and I continued to use some version of it off and on over the next couple of semesters.

Almost a year later I received a note from Miss Horse Jumper and she delightedly told me she had graduated, moved to North Carolina and was proudly working as the business manager of a large horse stable. She woke up each morning, took her horse for a few rounds, spent the day managing the stables, and then finished by giving lessons to young children.

She claimed the one moment I spoke to her in that small room about combining passion with talents changed her life forever. Little did she know, her letter changed mine and now perhaps thousands more. It was in that moment I truly realized the power of the message I carry. I became determined to refine, grow, and spread the message. The world needs to hear these stories and begin believing in the possibility of amazing again.

CONSTANT GROWTH (EVEN FOR ME)
The second quick story to pass along is brand new. By that, I mean, this section was added after the very first person read this book. Well at least a truly rough version of this book. I mean, she didn't even get cool graphics and worksheets. She is a coworker turned true friend and it was my honor for her to do a first read. I wanted her genuine feedback and knew

she would be honest. She provided lots of awesome comments you now get to benefit from. However, one specific comment really stuck with me.

This wonderful lady was sitting in Italy with her husband on a dream vacation. She was reading the chapter on creating bigger dreams and realized in that moment she wanted to find a way to move to Italy for a few months when she retires. Her comment was, "I found a passion in that moment I didn't even know I had".

That is what this book is about. I don't have a magical ability to give you the answers to your perfect path or life. I do, however, believe this book will show you where to look. Thanks again, Jen. Have fun and eat some pasta for me!

Chapter 4
How to Use this Book

"Change your thoughts and change your world"
-Norman Vincent Peale

This book is designed to drive you deep inside yourself. There will be no easy answers, and I can't provide them for you anyway. You must be the author of your life. The good news is everything you need to know is already inside you. You have known for a long time what your calling is. You have simply allowed outside voices to cloud your vision. This book is about stripping away all the noise and allowing your inner voice to speak out.

It is important to take your time with this book. Ideally, you read a chapter at a time and then take long pauses to contemplate the meaning of how it reflects in your life. Inevitably a time will come in the process the light switch will flip. You will feel the spark, sense the growing flame and want to rush ahead. You must fight this urge. Allow your instinct to guide you but remain committed to the process. By pacing yourself and allowing each area to sink in thoroughly before moving on you will dive deeper into your strength. It is critically important to remember that once you get this process right and the flame roars to life, you will be burning for the rest of your days. You have time. Do it right.

I expect people at all stages of life to find their way to this book. No matter where you find yourself currently you should start at the beginning of the book and work through it completely. I have forced myself to return to the topics of each area on a regular basis as it provides a way to strengthen the belief in myself and what I am doing with my life. There will never be a time in your life when remembering your worth, connecting with your calling, planning your path, and reflecting on the next steps is a bad thing.

Finally, I want to personally thank you. Thank you for taking steps to give the world your true talents. Thank you for seeking to change the world in a positive way. Thank you for trusting me enough to consider even starting the journey and using this map. Thank you for helping to validate my calling to help others find a better way forward. You are about to live an Authentic life and you have my eternal gratitude.

Let Your Fire Burn Until It Consumes All!

Part II:
The Awakening

Chapter 5
Choose Your Voice

"Life isn't about finding yourself. Life is about CREATING yourself"
-George Bernard Shaw

You aren't crazy. There really are voices in your head. A whole multitude of them. They all compete for your attention, and they all believe they are the most important. It's no wonder we find ourselves moving in fifty directions with no sense of purpose. There is no way to satisfy every voice we hear. It all becomes the "Noise".

From the time we are born we have an internal voice, your true voice, that knows exactly what it wants and what you should be doing with your life. The problem is over time more voices begin to shout out to us. Parents, teachers, friends, family, enemies, coaches, pastors, bosses, spouses and others all speaking for what they believe you should be doing. Worse are the internal voices you battle constantly. Fear, jealousy, pride and more begin eroding the confidence you have in your true voice. At some point all these voices begin to merge into one loud "Noise" that completely drowns out your tiny inner voice trying desperately to tell you the truth.

In this chapter I am asking you to set aside all other voices and focus only on the true voice inside your heart. To help you understand the various voices you are being exposed to, I would like to take a moment and explain an interesting way my wife reflects my voice back to me.

When I come up against a tough decision, I tend to get mired in looking at it from different angles. The angles reflect very specific roles I play in my life and the voices associated with them. I can be any of the following at any given moment.

Husband Jason
Father Jason

Son Jason
Brother Jason
Employee Jason
Boss Jason
Professor Jason
Friend Jason
Coach Jason ....and so on

Sarah will quickly redirect the question to, "what does Jason Jason" think is best. (To be clear she doesn't state it in those exact words because that would be weird.) There is no mention of what would be best for her as my spouse. What would be best for me as a dad? What would my parents expect of me? What would my family or boss think? She has enough faith in me to quietly ask, what does the true Jason believe is best?

This idea is critically important because only the decision my true self believes in will allow me to fully commit. There is not one single person on earth who has not experienced making a decision based on the voice of another, and then immediately regretting it. Most of the time we mutter to ourselves at some point in the future "I should have gone with my gut". Yes, you should have. You should also always go with your own voice moving forward. This is not an excuse to ignore other's feelings or your outside commitments. It is believing enough in yourself to know the true voice inside you would never allow harm to the ones you care about, value, and respect.

Time for your very first assignment. During this think session I want you to concentrate on identifying the voices that compete for space in your head. I want you to genuinely reflect on where those voices come from and what they are saying to and about you. Many of these will be negative and painful. That should be expected. It's also necessary.

Believe me, I hurt every time I go through this exercise. It is not fun to list things said about me. To repeatedly hear "you are a disappointment" from a parent. To hear "you talk too much" from hundreds of people. To hear "you are a quitter" from a boss you respect. To hear "I don't want you anymore" from a spouse. To hear "maybe I'd rather just die" from myself. All cutting to my core and leaving scars. Yet, all false.

This is your chance to write all those awful things said about you down. To give them life in a very real form and accept them as something said about you. Then it's your chance to kill them. To take all the power away from those words and voices as you allow your inner true voice to ring out loud with the TRUTH.

I respond to the terrible voices with my own voice of truth. I have only been disappointed in myself when I didn't follow my own path. I talk a lot because it's one of my talents and my students seem to appreciate that skill. I quit your job because it was slowly crushing my soul and I have not regretted it for one minute of my life. You may not want to be married anymore, but that's ok because I have amazing children as the re ward for our time together. I don't want to die. In fact, for the first time in my life I want to live fully everyday making a difference for others.

In the area below take the difficult and painful journey into the heart of the "Noise" and find your inner voice. You will know with certainty when you find it because it will ring with a truth you cannot deny.

VOICES IN MY HEAD

What are 5 painful things said about you and by whom? Focus on the repetitive, damaging ones used by people close to you.

1. _____

2. _____

3. _____

4. _____

5. _____

Now pull out your Sword of Truth and FIGHT BACK! Reword the criticisms to reflect a more accurate version of yourself.

1. _____

2. _____

3. _____

4. _____

5. _____

Chapter 6
Ignite the Spark

"The only journey is the one within."
-Rainer Maria Rilke

We are amazing creatures, us humans. We are the only animal on Earth that shapes its own destiny. We are self-aware and can act to change our situation. We are also perfectly unique. At a core level of DNA there is only one of you. You are the only you there has ever been. You are the only you there will ever be. Even "identical" twins are not truly identical in every single way. We maintain a uniqueness that cannot be tamed by society. This is something you should take great pride in. This world needs you to be YOU. There are things you can offer to the world that no one else can and no one will ever be able to. I will personally take great offense if you don't use your uniqueness to bring something incredible into the world. You will have robbed my family and I of seeing something awesome.

An outgrowth of this concept is your unique calling for life. You have a small piece of your purpose buried way down deep. During childhood it constantly found its way to the surface. You would show interest in unique things. You were drawn to activities you spent joyous hours on. Sadly, those days faded away and the voices of others began to dampen your flame. You were redirected to the path of normalcy. Told to think practical and stop acting like a child. Why? The child was the fun guy. The child was loving life because he was doing exactly what his voice told him he should be doing with his life.

For the next few minutes I want you to stop. No noise. No distractions. Just you and your thoughts. I want you to search inside and remember that Ember of your very being. That ONE reason for your existence. In the darkest moments of life, there must be ONE thing you can come back to. ONE tiny ember of the fire that can never be fully extinguished. You are an artist. You love nature. You want to defend the weak. You are a caregiver. What is it? That ONE thing is you at your purest form and it has the power to ignite a raging inferno of change. Name it. Right here. Right Now.

I MATTER BECAUSE ....

Once you have this Anchor you are ready to move forward. Allow me to name my tiny little spark so you can see how simple and yet powerful it can be.

I matter because I teach.

That's it. Simple. When everything around me is crashing down. When I reach my end point of frustration and fatigue. When I am tired and not sure if I have the energy or passion for the day. In those moments I reconnect with that tiny spark that tells me, "I matter because I teach". I want to make a positive impact on this world. My way of doing this is to teach.

In fact, I have crafted specific steps over the years to help me rekindle the fire and allow it to burn brightly when things get dark. These are the next steps for you.

I find tremendous power in identifying ways of rekindling my flame. For me there are a few techniques I would invite you to steal. The work section will give you a place to write all these down for your personal pick me up session.

- Song lyrics.

    There are few things in this world more powerful than music that touches you. For all of us there are songs that will change attitude and mood in an instant. I keep these at the ready. I even use them before I go speak publicly or teach to really fan the flames. In my case if it's Skillet, it's time to rock out and change the world. (*Easter Egg alert. If you look closely you will see song titles from Skillet sprinkled throughout this book.)

- Activities.

    I personally like to weight lift as a stress relief. If you like to run that's cool (my personal record for marathon distant is 0.0 miles☺). Play piano. Get your Mozart on. Cook like an at home chef. Please bring me some, I'm hungry. Whatever it is that allows you to decompress and reset is a good thing. Make time for it.

- Art in many forms.

    I have lines from movies I find awesome and motivating. I have poems that inspire me to be better.

I even look at something like a picture of Stonehenge and think, " thousands of years later and those people still matter". This is the beauty of art. It has an ability to speak to a place we can't articulate. Harness that power in whichever way works for you.

However you choose to stoke your flame is fine. In any case you should clarify exactly what methods will work for you. These will serve as a reference when the time comes, and you need the pick me up. On the following page give yourself some proven energy jolts.

FLAMETHROWERS

Song Lyrics: Write your favorite one-line lyrics from 2 songs that could serve as your theme music moving forward in life.

#1

Title_____

Artist_____

Lyrics_____

_____

_____

#2

Title_____

Artist_____

Lyrics_____

_____

_____

Poems and Literature:

Harness the words of writers that speak to your core desires. Below write the best lines from a powerful poem or literature piece

_____

_____

_____

_____

_____

Breaktime (and maybe breakdance if that is your thing)

Decide on 3 activities you are willing to COMMIT to which will help reset your mind and rekindle your flame

1. _____

2. _____

3. _____

KEEPER OF THE FLAME

The final piece once you have sparked the ember is to identify the one person who can be trusted to hold a tiny piece of your flame. This person serves to remind you of the truth and the promise you made to yourself. When things go sideways and you begin to hear the "Noise" so loudly you doubt yourself, this person will hold out a hand and show you a small piece of yourself. They will remind you of the strength inside and rekindle the flame.

Sarah does this for me all the time. She believes so completely in me, I am forced to be better. For reasons I can't figure out she has not realized I am an idiot. I work every day to keep her image of me alive. It's heartening and empowering to for her to be my Flame Keeper.

To make this process work to its fullest capacity you need to give serious thought to who can serve in this role. Keep in mind this will need to be someone who believes in you at your truest nature. For this reason, I believe parents are often a bad choice for Flame Keeper. As a parent myself I know the desire to see my children happy and safe. I also know no matter how hard I try; I will always have my dreams for them. I see things in them I wish they would strive for. I cringe when they make mistakes. In short, I am so invested in their life that I struggle to be objective and give them the space they need. This is not from lack of love, but the exact opposite.

You should aim for someone who will support you, challenge you, and ultimately has faith in you. This is not about faith in what you can do, but in just you. The real unfiltered you.

Write the name of person you intend to invite to take this role.

My Flame Keeper _____

Explaining to this person what exactly they have signed up for could prove challenging. Since I am not a **MONSTER,** I have prepared a few questions you can hand to this lovely human. Simply instruct them to ask these questions back to you when you are struggling. The questions are designed to re-center you on what matters at the core. If they are still confused tell them to call me. Better yet, have them read this book.

FLAME KEEPER CHALLENGE
QUESTIONS

1. Are you doubting yourself or allowing someone else's doubt to become your own?
2. Would this action be acceptable to the person you wish to become?
3. You said you matter because...........Does this action align with that statement?

Chapter 7
Set Standards

"It is far better to be alone, than to be in bad company."
-George Washington

There is beauty in simplicity. There is an ease in looking at something and knowing exactly what it represents. There is a comfort found when someone knows precisely what to expect from you. Children crave stability in the home. Spouses value a mate who can be relied upon to be consistent. As the world grows more and more complicated, we as humans continue to value simplicity.

Could this idea be applied to you? Have you established for yourself a straightforward, no nonsense, simple set of rules you live by? If not, why? What exactly is guiding your decision making? Can people count on you to be the same regardless of the situation? Do they know what to expect from you? More to the point, is what they expect of you positive?

We are nothing more than a collection of our habits and principles. We believe in a certain way of things and act accordingly. For the rest of this section we are going to look at what you can do to Set Standards for yourself. This will include harsh realities, as you will be forced to face the fact you haven't always stood by your professed principles. It will also be cathartic, as you are given permission to completely cut negative people from your life regardless of their biological connection.

Throughout this book we are going to cover four critical areas necessary for you to stand tall and take control of your own life.

- *Create a list of non-negotiables in your life.*

- *Spend a week tracking the actual time you spend on.....well....everything.*
- *Identification of non-productive habits you have formed.*
- *Creation of newly minted productivity habits. These include the all-powerful Keystone Habit.*

Now is the time for you to dig deep, look at your results in life to this point, and decide if maybe just maybe you have been a large part of the reason you aren't where you want to be. If the answer is yes (hint, it's always yes) then now would be a good time to break the pattern and **RISE UP**.

NOT NEGOTIABLE

The title of this piece is designed very specifically to drive home an emotion. I want you to say this loud and clear with me.

"I am not negotiable"

You are amazing exactly as you were designed. You have flaws, yes. You do stupid things all the time, yes. You can be selfish, irrational, and stubborn. Guilty on all counts. You can also be generous, kind, funny, and creative. Welcome to the human race. The key concept is very simply YOU MATTER. You have every right to set rules and standards for your life and those that wish to interact with you. This little section here is your chance to speak up and maybe lash out a little. Many times, in life you will face situations that cause you to question what you will tolerate in your world. Let's start with what you already know you won't tolerate. Let's create a list of items that simply are not up for debate in your little piece of the world.

***

The first three non-negotiables I ask you to consider should all be of the positive bent. By this I mean they can be stated in simple terms starting the sentence with something like "I will". If you prefer a more biblical slant to your vocabulary feel free to use "Thou Shall". It sounds more formal and makes you sound super smart. I want you to really drill down on those things which absolutely matter to you. You can be relied upon to ALWAYS do these given the chance. Let me give you a couple of mine to help you grease those mind skids.

- **I WILL focus my life on creating positive impact for others.** I want to spend my time trying to make this place a little better than I found it

- **I WILL force myself to have a bias towards action.** No waiting around and hoping something changes. You can ask my wife how well I keep to this (to her constant annoyance). I NEVER sit still.

- **I WILL accept others for who they are, exactly as they are in the moment.** It's not my job to change anyone else and I know the experience of being told something is wrong with you.

See that wasn't so hard was it. Your turn. Focus on the reasoning behind each item so you can deeply internalize the meaning.

I WILL _____

I WILL _____

I WILL _____

$$* * *$$

Now let's start cutting some crap from our lives. A part of the misery you feel in life is your failure to go do something you know you want to do. The other large anchor on your life is the constant overwhelming challenge of trying to avoid things you don't want to do. This moment right NOW is your permission to cut the cord. This time around you get to drive straight down into your best "I WILL NOT". Again, for my bible peeps, "Thou Shalt Not". Take some time and think through the core things in your life that are not making it better. What is your time drain? What saps your energy every time you engage in it? Are there types of people that leave you feeling a bit empty? See my examples to crank up your angst.

41

- **I WILL NOT ever work in a cubicle again.** You read my backstory. I was miserable in my former life and that single little gray prison cell represents all that I hate. I would rather be homeless and broke than return to that misery.

- **I WILL NOT spend time around people who are negative.** Pessimists. Yuck. They are simply the worst. Every moment I spend with these people drains away my energy and kind of my will to live. I make a very purposeful decision to turn and walk away when the negative hose gets turned on.

- **I WILL NOT pressure my children into the life I want for them.** Instead I will focus on supporting them to be whatever the hell it is they believe they should be. Ultimately if they are happy, I win.

Your turn. Now go throw up a middle finger at some stuff you no longer want in your life.

I WILL NOT

_____

_____

I WILL NOT

_____

_____

I WILL NOT

_____

_____

Chapter 8
Expect Amazing

"Keep your face always towards the sunshine and the shadows will fall behind you."
-Walt Whitman

Your goals for life are too small. I can say that almost universally. For some reason we have stopped believing in amazing. We only hope for basic things and are satisfied living an unsatisfying life. We respond to questions about our *dreams* with mundane, normal, BORING goals.

- *I want to buy a house someday.*
- *I want to have a family.*
- *I want to find a job that pays me enough to eat.*
- *I'd like to travel to Paris one day.*
- *I'd like to buy a new SUV.*

Are you seriously kidding me with this stuff? When we were children, we dreamed the right way.

- *Someday I'm going to be an astronaut.*
- *I will grow up and be President of the United States.*
- *I'm going to be a doctor and cure cancer, so no more mommies have to die.*
- *I will win a Nascar race.*
- *I will start a doggy daycare so I can play with all the cute little puppies everyday.*
- *I will sit in the stands as the Cleveland Browns win their first Superbowl. (Maybe if I throw this out into the world, the universe will take pity on me☺)*

Man, our kid versions were so much cooler. They had real dreams to change the world. Why? Simple, no one told them they couldn't. Well, I'm telling you now the same thing. Today. Right now. You must expand your dreams. You need to strive for more in your life. You need to set an expectation of amazing from this moment forward.

I know you can't see my vision board because it's hanging on my office wall at home. Well, if you can see it then we need to have a discussion about personal boundaries. In either case, I want to lay out my vision board for you so you can see the expansion process. Let's start with the sad, small, uninspired dreams I had only a matter of a few years ago.

- *I wanted to teach at a college*
- *I wanted to provide a solid home for my children to grow and become their best selves*
- *I wanted to take my wife oversees on a "trip of a lifetime"*

My major issue with these goals? They are far too small. In fact, by the time I was 38 I had already accomplished all of them. That is just sad. Am I done now? Is it sort of cruise control for the next 50 years? How does this work? It works by expanding your dreams until they are scary and hard. My new vision board looks like this.

- I have a huge picture of a beach house. Why? Easy, that's where my wife and I are going to live as soon as my kids move out.

- There is a picture of a giant arena full of people. I have come to believe in my message and its importance so much that teaching classes is not enough. I want to spread the message to larger audiences. Large enough to even scare someone with no fear of public speaking like me.

- There is a picture of the world map. I don't want to travel to a specific place. I want to travel and experience all of them. In fact, I would not mind living oversees for a time. In either case, my passion for traveling must be fed with a huge goal. I went so far with this goal that I had a giant map tattooed on my forearm. A constant reminder of living every day for a bigger goal.

- Lastly, there are pictures of an awesome bakery and a car dealership. I don't have a passion for either of these things (well ok, I do love the doughnuts), but I do have a passion for my children's future. My son is obsessed with cars and wants to own a dealership. I will invest enough to get him started. My daughter is in love with everything about baking. I will buy her a bakery, turn her passion loose, and create a doughnut empire.

I tell you these things because I want to show that dreaming big has a way of driving new decisions and pushing away fear. There is no room to be afraid or timid in your approach to life if you have audacious goals. In working your way through the vision board process, you will truly capture and crystallize your amazing future life. You will find it leads to you living an amazing NOW life as well.

Homework Project: Arts and Crafts Time

Before you move on, I want you to create your vision board. I don't care if you use an electronic version or a real-life poster. Only rules I care about are it must be audacious, and it must be visible to you on a constant basis. Go forth and create your best art project.

Part III:

The Convergence Point

How do people find that one true calling in life? Does everyone have a calling? Why are some people so annoyingly happy all the time? Are the drugs they use legal? We have all asked ourselves these questions at one point or another. The truth is we are capable of an amazing life, lived doing exactly what we are great at. It boils down to finding that path as soon as possible, and then committing wholly to it.

This section of the book is called the Convergence Point because I strongly believe your best possible life sits firmly in the spot where the things you love (obsessions), the reason you act (motivations), and the areas in which you are naturally gifted (talents) come together.

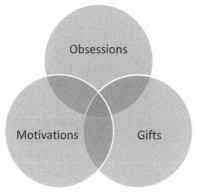

Come with me to dreamy future land. Imagine a life where you wake up every day excited about heading to a job where you make the difference YOU want to make in the world, using YOUR unique skills in a field YOU love. That should be the true American Dream. It's also entirely possible. In fact, it should be the only goal. What is your alternative? A job you hate. A company and industry you don't enjoy or have passion for. A life spent ignoring your special talents. That all sounds awful. Instead journey with me to a place of personal joy where you do MATTER. Very much in fact. The place of convergence.

Chapter 9
Finding Inspiration

"Take up one idea. Make that one idea your life - think of it, dream of it, live on that idea. Let the brain, muscles, nerves, every part of your body, be full of that idea, and just leave every other idea alone. This is the way to success."

-Swami Vivekananda

A wise man (or woman, frankly I am too lazy to look it up) once said find something you love and then find a way to make money doing it. I couldn't support this idea any more strongly. Far too many people have allowed themselves to slip into a world of mediocrity and meaningless work. The kind of work that does nothing for your soul and uses none of your inborn talents. This is an absolute shame as we all have amazing things to offer the world.

The challenge is in finding what direction we should even begin heading. Think of this chapter as a compass. I have no idea where you are headed, but you do. Allow the questions and ponderings of this chapter to identify your North Star. That core group of things that calibrate your compass and set you on the right path.

I think it's important to start by explaining what I mean by your inspiration and obsession. These terms have become so widely used in society they are losing meaning. Perhaps just as important is what I don't mean.

- **Inspiration (Websters)** - *An influence directly and immediately exerted upon the mind and soul.*

- **Inspiration (Jason)** - *something that gives you all the "feels and tingles"*

- **Obsession (Websters)** - *the domination of one's thoughts or feelings by a persistent idea or desire*

- **Obsession (Jason)** - *uh, actually I will go with Webster on this one☺*

Those are the literal definitions of the words. We are aiming for those very few things in your life that constantly occupy space in your brain. You can't turn them off. You daydream about them. You OBSESS over them (duh). For this reason, I want to take a moment and eliminate one large word from this list and not allow anyone to use it.

FAMILY

Yikes, did this guy just say I can't be inspired by my family? No, I didn't. Of course, people in your family can be an inspiration. They can't, however, be your obsession. You don't think about your family all day. You don't dream about them as a life goal. If you say you do, you are lying. I have presented this program live more times than I can count. Every time I ask the question about what people are truly inspired by, it's societal habit to say family. This is why I changed the question to what are you obsessed with? This way answering family........ just sounds a little creepy.

To really clarify this point, I have listed my Obsessions below. Don't judge me.

1. *Traveling and Exploring*
2. *Learning and Education*
3. *Change - creating new and different in all forms*

There is one last key thing to note before I move you on to questions designed to help you target in on your obsession. See how I only listed 3 things above. Yeah, that was on purpose. If you get farther down the list, then three you are talking about things that mildly interest you. That is not helpful for this exercise. Focus on only three. My guess is these will come quickly because, by definition, you were already thinking about them all the time.

***

To get started I want you to take time and answer each of the following questions. Extra space provided for your enjoyment.

1. What do you get truly upset about? I mean, what just fires you up? People do not get worked up and upset about things that don't deeply matter to them. Take the time to drill down on this topic. If political hot buttons get you upset, make sure you identify specifically what it is. It's very unlikely (though maybe for some) you care about "politics". More likely you care about one area being debated on the national stage. Maybe you get fired up about local causes or certain injustices you see in the world. Take the time to flesh this out and try to really understand the core of what is angering you.

_____

_____

_____

_____

2. What can you talk about for hours? There is always a topic that seems to come up in every conversation with you. For me it doesn't take very long into our talk before I am asking about your passions and whether you are enjoying life. Most of the time I am not even consciously trying to steer the conversation this way. It has just become such an important topic in my life that I can't help but ask at some point. Think about the types of things you discuss with people on a regular basis. Is there a hint in those talks about the kind of things you are passionate about?

_____

_____

_____

_____

3. Who is your role model? Have you ever stopped to think about why they are? Sometimes it can be their morals and how they stick to them. It could be their career success. It could be the obstacles they

overcame. Analyze your connection to the role model and what it is about them that really speaks to you.

_____

_____

_____

_____

4. Time for a trip down memory lane. When you were a child what types of things did you love to do? The child you was not constrained by society to be more "realistic". You were free to explore, invent games, and generally engage in anything that sparked your interest. What was it? During my childhood my parents packed me up and shipped me off via airplane to my grandparents in Texas on a number of occasions. I remember these trips as simply amazing. I loved everything about the experience. I vividly remember the joy and wonder of getting on a plane in cold Ohio and a couple hours later arriving in a whole new world of warm Texas. To this day I am still obsessed with traveling and experiencing new places and cultures. Now it is your turn to reflect back on your best memories and the things that truly brought you joy as a child. Your passion is in those memories.

_____

_____

_____

_____

5. Is there something you would do for free? I would teach for free. (Please don't tell my department chair this fact). I truly love interacting with my students and watching them discover a new side of themselves. It brings me enough internal satisfaction that I would do it for free if asked. Turns out that passion has made me good enough that I get paid handsomely to do the thing I enjoy. Can you think of some "jobs" you would do for free because of the deep satisfaction they bring you?

_____

_____

_____

_____

6. Last one. You just won the Powerball jackpot. 500 million big buckaroos. Now what? It's really that

simple. When people remove the pressures of a "normal" life such as paying bills and housework, their true passions have room to roam. I want you to place yourself in that headspace. All the pressure of having a job because you need to eat is gone. You now have enough money in the bank to play poker with God. What does tomorrow look like for you? For me it's easy. My children, wife, and I are now free to travel the entire world and explore all the amazing things this planet has to offer (when they aren't in school of course). I get to volunteer teach and give lectures about career passion on my schedule. When the time comes my children own any business that brings them fulfillment in their lives. This crystal-clear picture of my perfect life shows with absolute certainty where my obsession is. So, what does your "rich like Bill Gates" life look like?

_____

_____

_____

_____

The answers to these questions should start to bring clarity to your preferred life. I ask that you hold tight to these answers. They will serve as a guidepost for your future. If you begin down a path that does not involve a true, deep inside passion you are headed for a life of low satisfaction.

Chapter 10
Catalyst

"All our dreams can come true, if we have the courage to pursue them."

-Walt Disney

We all have motivations. We all have our reasons for doing things. In the end we are all rats trying to get the cheese at the end of a maze. We want rewards. The beauty of this is the reward that matters most to each of us is extremely unique. For some it can be money. For some it's fame. Others, it could be finally getting to tell all your doubters to shove it. There is no shortage of motivational drivers in the world.

This chapter will give you headspace to identify what really drives you. What I am looking for when this is all done is a mission statement. Sounds hokey right? Well it is, but it also works really well. It's not that a mission statement suddenly aligns the Stars and provides you with constant daily inspiration. It's far more about the process of creating the mission statement. If you can't honestly say why you make the decisions you do in life, you have no direction. We need to fix that. Take some time and answer the following questions.

***

1. What do you wish for people to say about you at your funeral? Is being a good accountant enough? Gross. How about, "He worked 15 hours every day until he died"? Really gross. Wouldn't it be better to live a life where you are remembered as a loyal friend, a committed father, someone who revived a dying town, someone who explored the world, an educator who changed the lives of children, or some other amazing accolades. What is your eulogy?

_____

_____

_____

_____

2. What do you personally view as a reward for a job well done? Do you want more money? (Btw, its ok to admit this. Money is fun.) Do you want fame? Do you want the respect of your peers? Do you want more free time? You need to determine what reward would actually motivate you on a daily basis.

_____

_____

_____

3. Are you trying to model your life for someone else? Do you view your decisions as impacting someone else? If someone looks up to you, what do you want them to see? What kind of person do you want them to become? This matters because it will impact your decisions and your motivations for life. A huge part of my decision to leave

the soul sucking corporate job was the impact I believed it would have on my children in the future. I preach to them about becoming the best they can and doing something they love. I was a hypocrite. I hated my job and was miserable. Only by taking a stand and leaving that job could I model the life I wanted for them. Who are you modeling for and what do you want them to see?

_____

_____

_____

4. Are there things that do not motivate you at all? Just because the world says money and titles matter doesn't make it so. Those could mean nothing to you. It is just as important to understand what doesn't drive you. Otherwise, you will find yourself chasing dreams others have. When you think of the "rewards" typically associated with successful lives, are there some that hold no appeal to you? In some ways this can be critically helpful to your future dreams. If more pay is not important to you, would your boss be willing to offer more vacation as a trade-off? The reality is most bosses assume you want money. If this isn't true, then let them know so they can make you happy.

_____

_____

_____

***

Now I would ask you to begin the process of crafting a mission statement. For the purpose of aiding you along I will provide mine. Keep in mind this will be completely personal and should give you clear guidance when any decision comes up in your life.

I will work each day to make the lives of those around me better. I will show the next generation how capable they are, and how big their impact can be.

Your Mission

_____

_____

_____

_____

Chapter 11
The Real YOU

"Everybody is a genius. But if you judge a fish by its ability to climb a tree, it will live its whole life believing that it is stupid."

-Albert Einstein

Have you ever noticed that we seem to have an obsession with smart people? The ones who we claim, "make everything look easy". What we mean in most cases is they make school in the traditional sense look easy. We mistake the idea of being "book smart" (which is itself a strange term) with being intelligent. This simply isn't true. Yes, there are many people who do well in school and then do well in life. This shouldn't come as a shock to anyone. Yet, there are plenty of people who were not good at schoolwork and then go on to lead remarkable lives. How can this be? The people who didn't do well in school are dumb, right? Not even close.

A huge part of helping you find the true natural strengths you possess is clearing up the misinformation about intelligence. Intelligence type, learning ability, learning style, and the generic "smartness" are far too complicated to be measured in one simple exercise like a standardized test. This is a multifaceted topic that requires us to understand variations in us as humans. Let's explore a few ideas as we move forward.

THINKING ABOUT THINKING

We can start with the two main types of thinking. These being Convergent and Divergent thinking. To understand these is to reflect on kids you grew up with and realize many of them were far smarter than you gave them credit for.

Schools in the United States focus almost entirely on the type of intelligence known as convergent intelligence.

This is your natural ability to take known facts, process or "converge" them in some way, and generate a correct response. This is basically every academic class you have taken in your life. Math classes provide a formula, give you raw data, and tell you to provide the one correct answer.

Those with a convergent mind can master these concepts more easily and will in time develop skills that allow them to do this with relative ease. These are the students we call "smart". We only call them this, however, because standardized tests, by definition, must have a correct answer. Therefore, this specific type of intelligence is favored in our educational system.

This type of intelligence is also largely correlated with what we call a person's IQ. IQ testing is again a system based on puzzle solving in which there is a correct answer. Therefore, the same people are preferred.

This causes a long-term effect in which a certain type of person with a specific intelligence type is highlighted as "skilled" and "smart". They rise to the top of their school class and the expectation is they will be successful in life. The problem is real life doesn't follow a formula.

***

The second type of intelligence is Divergent thinking. This type of "smart" looks at a person's ability to take some known fact, object, product, etc. and view it in a completely different way. Essentially, it's breaking apart the known and trying to create something entirely different. This skill is important to provide alternative paths forward, create new things, develop art, and problem solve. Interestingly, it's a skill that is imperative to a large part of the American spirit of ingenuity and entrepreneurship. Yet, we don't value it as highly. At the very least we don't formally recognize it in our educational system. We want conformity, not individuality. This causes the people who are strong in this area to feel like outsiders.

It is important to remember that neither type of intelligence is "better". Our society needs all people to be involved. Every project requires some creativity to generate new ideas. However, it also requires those with strong analytics to make sure it's achievable.

There is no reason to be proud of your intelligence type. There is also no reason to be ashamed of it. You are you. Perfect as you are. We as a collective simply need you to acknowledge the truth of your inner "smarts" so we can harness it.

YOUR LEARNING STYLE

Our second major classification for dividing "smart" people from the rest is learning style. This dscribes the way a person absorbs or learns new material and skills. There have been many studies done on this area and most agree the major styles are Visual, Verbal, and Kinesthetic. In addition, you can be sub-divided into either a social learner or solitary learner. Almost everyone is a combination of these classes, but most people have a strong natural preference for one area.

Our school system in America is based largely on a class of students (social) sitting face forward having a teacher talk at them (Verbal). Occasionally the teacher will throw in some slides or other visual materials. Rarely do most school children have the opportunity to choose how or what they will learn. Rarely are they allowed to use hands on experiments to develop skills. Normally this is reserved for science class.

In what should be a surprise to no one, we have developed a very specific type of "good" student. It's a social person who likes to talk, learns by listening and occasionally see things on the screen. If you mix this with the Convergent analytical thinker, you arrive at the perfect student. These students get A grades and are promoted as the best we have in society.

This mix of child fails to address a massive percentage of our population though. We leave behind children who enjoy using their hands to learn. Those who like to explore and tinker and experiment. We ignore those who want self-directed learning. We set aside the children who challenge the status quo and create new art. These types of learners are all considered outliers and told they have other special types of skills. Code words for "you aren't smart enough to hang with the cool kids". The reality is they simply don't fit the very narrow box of skills needed to succeed in our regimented educational system.

Why do I bring all of this to your attention? Simple. I want each and every person to realize they are smart in their own right. Equally powerful in your abilities with your peers you were told were perfect because they scored well on some tests the state gave them.

As you begin to take a serious inventory of your natural talents, I want you to drill down past the labels and mundane "skills" you have been conditioned to believe in. You should be focusing on those very unique core talents you possess that allow you to rise above your peers.

It is also important for you to know how you need to learn material. Every path you choose for your life will require you to become a master. This means there will be loads of things to learn. The entire exercise of moving towards mastery of your chosen field will be easier if you clearly understand for yourself how you best learn things. The next section will begin asking the questions to help you learn who you are.

PERSONALITY COMPLEX

Every human is a mix of conflicting ideas and values. There is no person who is absolute in their ways. You are ALWAYS honest? Really. Did you celebrate Christmas, including Santa, with your children when they were younger? You are always frugal? Did you answer yes while sitting in your Victoria Secret sweatshirt and Nike shoes? This is not to say that we as humans don't have tendencies. Of course we do. We are born with certain personality traits that influence all our decisions. As with your intelligence type, you have a "normal" way of operating. This is the important piece of information to learn about yourself. The foundational exercise to this entire journey is finding a life path that will take advantage of everything you already are. A large piece of what you are is your personality.

In order to ensure you wander into a career or path well suited to your nature, you must take the time to understand the various pieces and parts of who you are. The exercise you will undertake for this chapter is a 120-question survey designed by people far smarter than I am. This survey will breakout how you stand on the 5 key domains of Personality. I am asking you to take the longer version (there are tests with 40 questions) because this allows a further refining of additional subcategories under the Big 5. Go to the following site and fire away.

http://www.personal.psu.edu/~j5j/IPIP/ipipneo120.htm

Quickly, lets cover what the Big 5 personality traits are and some helpful reminders of how to use the results.

1. **Extroversion** - Do you enjoy being included in social settings? Is your preference to be in the spotlight. Is this a good thing or bad thing? It depends on what you would like to do as a career.
2. **Agreeableness** - Are you someone who shows high levels of empathy and kindness? Do you trust other people by nature? These are things you can learn about yourself.
3. **Conscientiousness** - Are you organized and disciplined? Do you get your work done on time? Do you show impulse control?

4. **Neuroticism** - What are your feelings about yourself? Are you nervous most of the time? Are you confident? Do you consider yourself an optimist or pessimist?
5. **Openness** - Do you value creativity and art? Do you like change? Are you willing to try new things or value tradition?

To be clear, there is no "better" way to be on any of these scales. They are simply a reality in which you live. You must learn these traits about yourself because many jobs require different traits. Here are my thoughts on using the results.

You are who you are. You can spend a great deal of time trying to modify for what you believe to be the better. This is an admirable goal, and I support self-improvement in every way. What you cannot do is undercut generations of biological programming at your core.

If you are a natural introvert, you won't wake up one day and suddenly want to give a speech in front of a thousand people. It doesn't mean you are not capable of accomplishing this task. Hard work can do wonders. You likely won't ever truly enjoy it though. I say this because ultimately, setting up your life to achieve great things requires daily effort and multiple failures over time. You are far more likely to stay the course if you truly enjoy what you are trying to accomplish.

So how do we read these results? I think it best to look to the extremes. Remember when I asked you a couple paragraphs ago to take the longer version. I did this because it breaks your larger traits into smaller pieces on a scale of 1-100. You should focus on the items that score 0-20 or 80-100.

Why? These represent areas you are pretty definitive about. If a job will require something that falls in your 0-20 range, you need to jump ship immediately. This is a terrible fit. If a task relies on something you score a 90 on, then full steam ahead. Odds are high you will love that challenge because it plays to your nature.

As an example, I am an extreme extrovert. I enjoy social settings and don't mind being the center of attention. These traits have led me to completely embrace my time as a professor. These same traits should have steered me far away from my job as a controller. Sitting in an office by myself for hours was basically daily torture. In addition, I am off the scales on Openness. I truly enjoy change and creativity. I like variety and shaking things up. I am, however, very low on the specific area of Conscientiousness that deals with details. Strangely people don't like their accountants to attempt being "creative". They also like the numbers within the financial reports to, well you know, be accurate and stuff.

In summary, you want to know yourself well, without being too critical of your perceived weaknesses. Life is about setting yourself up with opportunities that play to your natural strengths as often as possible. This increases the likelihood of you winning and enjoying the ride to get there.

WHO ARE YOU?

-List the results of your test by highs and lows

Top 3 Personality Traits (things your job should absolutely include)

1. _____

2. _____

3. _____

Top (wait, maybe its bottom) 3 traits to avoid in a job

1. _____

2. _____

3. _____

Hint – screen every possible opportunity in your life against these results. No amount of convincing yourself will change the truth. If it's a bad match, it's a bad match. Live with it and move on.

GO DO YOU

It's time to rock out to the amazing YOU. There are things inside you just waiting to burst out. Gifts you were given that other people simply do not possess. Have you ever stopped to think about the areas of your life that come easy to you? No, you haven't. Why? Because the world has become obsessed with telling us to work on our weaknesses. This is terrible advice. Nothing incredible in this world ever happened because someone went from being awful at something to being merely bad. Even progressing to mildly crappy or mediocre is still far below the standard required of awesome.

I am a terrible singer (my family and most people at my gym can attest to this). This is never going to change. No matter how much effort I pour into it, I will still be a dying cat trying to claw his way out of a coffee can. Guess what. Who cares? I am paid a whole bunch of money to utilize my unique skill in communications. I have been gifted with an ability to distill difficult information into digestible chunks and the confidence to do so in front of large groups of people. These abilities allow me to excel as a college professor as well as public speaker. Even my long-ago childhood criticism of talking too much was actually a unique skill. It turns out people like their public speakers to, you know, actually talk a lot. In any case, my point is you can stop worrying about the things you are not "good" at. They frankly don't matter.

Where weaknesses do come into play is in your filtering process. By identifying the areas you are not strong in, you gain a head start on eliminating work that is not right for you. As mentioned, I am NOT a detail person in the slightest. Strangely, I couldn't figure out why I was miserable in my former job as a corporate controller. You know, just the person charged with reviewing EVERY SINGLE DETAIL on the financial statements. Yikes. Who screwed up and let me have this job? Oh wait, I did. It was my responsibility to know my strengths and weaknesses better, and to opt out of this type of job. Now, it's your turn.

You are going to spend some time drilling down into your skill set. As you get started there are some questions to ponder and some examples of "bad" skills. By bad skills I mean bad examples for you to consider your own. You will see what I mean shortly, stay with me.

Questions to ask yourself on this journey down the rabbit hole.

1. What kinds of things come easy to you that others fear? We all have special areas where fear doesn't weigh us down. I truly enjoy public speaking. For most people that is their version of a nightmare. In fact, it is the number one cited fear among Americans. This one trait gives me a huge potential advantage. What is yours?

2. Is there something you are constantly getting compliments for? The odds are very good people are not complementing your artwork because it's crappy. Other people have no issue recognizing things they like. Sometimes you are too close to the situation and need the feedback of others to see clearly.

3. I need to hire you for ONE job. Your choice. This is your only chance to impress me and land the dream position at my amazing company. What are you going

to do for me? What is the one thing where you have so much confidence you would be willing to push all your chips to the middle of the table? I have already made it clear about my ability to speak publicly with confidence. There is zero question this is where I would place my faith. You have that. What is it?

4. Next is a silly offshoot of number three. You get to go on America's Got Talent and compete for 1 million dollars. This is your shot. What are you bringing to the stage? Are you gifted at puzzles? How about problem solving? Great artist? Can you organize the crap out of a room? Did you plan the most amazing party ever? Dig deep because this is the key to your superpowers.

5. Is there something you are capable of grinding through that others can't tolerate? If you are capable of sitting still and processing detailed information over a long period of time, congratulations. You are far more qualified for some jobs then I am. Can you listen to people complain without wanting to punch them? You can be a therapist:)

6. When do you feel in the "flow"? This term refers to those special few moments when everything in your world aligns. You find incredible energy; your talents rise to the surface and you simply know it's all working. Athletes express it as being in the zone. I find my moments of flow after a couple minutes on stage.

Maybe yours is when the music is pumping, and you are studying bacteria under a microscope. Maybe it's when the paint begins hitting the canvas and you forget about the rest of the world while you simply create. Whatever it is for you, remember it. Embrace it. This is the key to understanding how you unlock your full power.

To give you some additional insight, I am including another online survey. This was also designed by smarter people than me. I believe you should use the results of this survey to confirm what you already know in your heart. Go forth and survey.

https://high5test.com/

***

As promised, I want to address some "bad" examples of talents. I don't mean it is not good to have these skills. I mean they are too vague to be of use in identifying your dream future.

- *Any kind of being good at a subject.* Saying you are good at "math" is pointless. Do you mean you are good at problem solving? Following formulas? Doing multiplication? Analyzing complex data sets (which would be a great skill btw). What specifically do you mean? These weak, subject based, talents are a major cause of the epidemic we find ourselves in currently.

Too many school guidance counselors recommend careers based on grades we receive in certain subjects. I was a perfect example. Straight A's in math. Oh, he must be an accountant. They use numbers. Yes, except I hate details. I hate being stuck at a desk in an office. I hate routine work. This was a huge mismatch of my personality and job. Don't fall for this overly vague "talent" label.

- *Hard working is not a skill or talent.* Everyone claims to be hard working, until they aren't. Every person will magically be a better worker when they love what they do.

- *Lastly, avoid positive traits.* Things like loyal, caring, good listener, responsible etc. are all positive traits to strive for in life. They are not talents. You cannot make a living as a "loyal" person. I can't hire you to be "responsible".

As you finalize these talents for yourself keep in mind that you should focus on about 4-5 max. You want to truly be the best at something in order to make a difference. We want to avoid watering down your talent pool here. (Hold on, can you water down a pool? Why do we say that?) Also, try to think more conceptually about specific areas in which you are just different. Here is my list to help you along.

- **Organizing and planning.** I get a true kick out of planning a project. I look at every step, every possible outcome, every needed resource. I am able to look at the final needed outcome and backwards plan to exactly what my team needs to be doing at each stage. My wife and coworkers think I might have a clinical problem with Excel and list making. I showed them a very organized spreadsheet explaining why I think they are wrong☺

- **Communication of complex ideas.** I am comfortable taking large concepts and breaking them down into digestible chunks. This combined with my comfort of public speaking allows me to be a positive college teacher. It also allows me to write books. You know, like the one you are reading.

- **Divergent problem solving.** I am not interested in what everyone already knows. I am more concerned with breaking things apart and creating something new. This book is an example of that. Everything written here is contained in more detail in other books I have come across. What I hope to do is take bits and pieces from different sources and reimagine them in a unique way that allows you to have your "aha" moment.

Bonus good news. If you want to supercharge your future, then look to combine interesting but different skills you already have.

I am classically trained (read college educated) in finance. I understand the concepts and formulas. I am what I would describe as perhaps slightly above average in my skills regarding finance. I openly confess there are many peers in the field FAR smarter and amazing at finance then I am. However, I also possess a unique ability to explain complex things in a clear way for others to follow. I have spent years honing this skill presenting to School Boards. I discovered I don't need to be the best school finance person in the world. I need to supercharge that skill with a talent I possess that very few others in my field do. I work hard to craft my little niche of the world as the guy who can come in and explain in clear and simple terms how to improve the school's financial situation. My career has grown even as my financial knowledge stays essentially the same. This same supercharged skill set is what ultimately led me to become a professor. You don't need to be the brightest mind in your field to teach freshman college students. You need to be able to explain concepts in a way they can learn. Try looking for your combination superpower.

Chapter 12
Convergence of YOU

"Today you are you! That is truer than true! There is no one alive who is you-er than you!"
-Dr. Seuss

Now is your time. You have spent time learning what passions are burning inside you. You have a better understanding of what motivates and drives you in this life. Lastly, you found your superpowers. The final step is to take all the ingredients and throw them in a blender. The cocktail that emerges is your Convergence. It's the place in the world where you are the best version of you.

I constantly remind my students this information is the most powerful filter you will ever possess. No opportunity, job offer, volunteer assignment, or other life choice should enter your world without being filtered through this knowledge of yourself. It will take time to find the exact "life path" that fits your perfect convergence. While that process plays out, it becomes even more important you do not allow the wrong opportunities to enter your path. It is truly amazing to harness the power of a simple "No". Don't give air to ideas and choices that will take you farther away from the core of who YOU truly are.

As you think your way through possible options for your future, I want you to keep in mind three key ingredients to any successful long-term career:

1. Complexity
2. Autonomy
3. Connection between work and rewards

It will be hard to craft and enjoy a long career in any position missing these elements. Let's quickly scan the three components to make sure you understand what you are looking for.

COMPLEX BY DESIGN

Complexity sounds like a bad thing for a job. This is true if you are looking for an easy job that requires no brain power and you are fine being bored after about 2 days. My guess, since you are reading this book, is you are not interested in the boring route. You want to challenge yourself to something higher in life. In order to remain engaged in your job for a long period of time it needs to include some complexity. You need to be mentally challenged to push your limits. The job needs to change and evolve. You should face different obstacles on a regular basis. This changing landscape will keep your mind nimble and engaged. It will give you space to improve and grow along with the career. It will also open doors for you to find unique opportunities. Routine, mundane work simply lacks all these options. Don't be afraid of a complex job. Embrace it.

YOU ARE NOT THE BOSS OF ME

I know this may come as a shock, but most people don't like having a boss look over their shoulder all the time. No one likes to be constantly under the microscope and be told EXACTLY what to do. When you first start your career, it makes sense to value guidance and advice from mentors and bosses. It can be a tremendous growth opportunity to be subjected to constant scrutiny as you learn to master your craft. At a certain point, however, you need to gain autonomy. You need the chance to direct your own path. This does not only apply to those who wish to start their own business. Even workers at large corporations crave the opportunity to have true input on their job. People want to help decide on the goals of the position. People want to be given latitude as to how the job gets done. Ultimately you must search out a career path where your increasing skills can be matched with increasing freedom to do as you see best. Innovation can't be accomplished in an environment where people are not allowed the chance to spread their wings and try things in their own way. Your goal is to seek out a life path where you maintain the control over your life and your job.

OVER HERE JUST SAVING THE WORLD

The final piece of a successful career seems straight forward. You should choose a path where your work is directly tied to your rewards. It seems easy, but most jobs fail this simple test of connection. Take a moment and think back on many of the jobs you have had. Was there TRULY a connection between the work you put in and pay or rewards you received? I am not talking about hoping for future raise that might not come. I mean a true and direct connection from the work you accomplish today to the rewards you reap. I am not talking only about money as far as rewards. It can be whatever motivates you. Here's a hint. We addressed what really motivates you a few chapters ago during the Catalyst section. Every career opportunity you find yourself facing must be viewed through the lens of connection to rewards. Make sure you choose a path where you know without question each day of work will drive direct rewards. This simple step will keep you engaged for the long haul.

***

To put a final bow on this idea, let's look at the occupation often associated with high job and life satisfaction coupled with longevity. Teachers. Why are they always so happy? Well, time for a breakdown.

Teachers clearly face a complex job. They have kids in their classroom who all face different challenges in learning. They must meet the targets of multiple different testing structures. Many are teaching different subjects. As the year moves along, they teach different topics. All of this equals complexity. First box checked off.

Next, teachers are given latitude to adapt their lesson plans to meet the needs of their students. The way they handle the classroom is largely within their control. Even the decor in the room is largely their choice. Autonomy, and second box checked off. (*warning to our nation. We are creating ever more requirements for our teachers that strip away their autonomy. The result is a drop in job satisfaction and severe teacher shortage. We must remember a critical piece of keeping teachers happy and satisfied is trusting them enough to let them do their job.)

The final step is to connect work with reward. Most teachers did not enter the field for the money. Instead, there was passion for helping kids. It is difficult to have a more direct connection of work and reward then teaching a child new material and seeing the immediate reward of them learning it. As a teacher myself I can speak to the powerful impact of seeing the light come on for a student. The effort I pour into teaching also brings long term rewards as I see students years later and they have grown and matured into a success. I was part of that. It motivates me to teach the next student. Box three checked off and a career well lived.

Below, I would like you to simply list 3 POSSIBLE options for your path forward. You will know something belongs on this list if you light up immediately upon thinking of it. Where does your Convergence happen?

1. _____

2. _____

3. _____

Part IV:

UNLEASHED

Okay Mr. Bigshot, you have managed to complete the first two sections of this journey. Impressive. However, in case you didn't notice you have not actually DONE anything. That changes starting now. It is super important to develop a belief in yourself. It is also critical to understand the path your career should begin down. Those are guideposts pointing you in the right direction. Now you need to put on your shoes and actually begin walking the path.

This section is called **UNLEASHED** because you are no longer tethered to society's view of you and what you are "supposed" to be. You are going to go where you believe best from this point forward.

"Light a Match
Leave the past
Burn the Ships, and don't you look back"

-For King and Country

Chapter 13
Plan to Focus by Focusing on the Plan

"The secret of getting ahead is getting started."
-Mark Twain

A quick note of background as we proceed. The entire book you are reading began as nothing more than a one class lecture to my students on what you know as The Convergence Point. It wasn't called that at the time, but that doesn't matter. It was an immediate success and many students for many semesters would come up to me afterwards excited about the change in mindset and potential for their future. They all had the same question. Now what? In my short sightedness I had given no thought to how I would help them use the information gathered about themselves to make immediate changes.

I began working on this section as a way to give students a map for moving forward with the career of their dreams. The experiences of these young people helped craft the road map being presented here for you. It is critically important to understand this is where the rubber meets the road and you begin to see change in your life.

My first comment to every student who seeks to take this adventure to the next stage is, "are you focused?". Followed quickly by, "what is your plan?". These seems like basic questions. In fact, they are. There is nothing earth shattering about the concepts. People have been planning goals and focusing on them for generations. Correction. Successful people have been doing this. That's the whole point. The issue comes down to how you set yourself up in the best possible way to achieve focus and execute the plan. I do unsurprisingly have thoughts on this.

There are about 5,000 goal planning workbooks, phone apps, websites, etc. available to everyone. I am not looking to recreate a step by step on how to plan for your future. I would highly recommend you use these tools as they are powerful and can give you great guidance on the process. It's just not what you and I are working on right now. What I am looking to clarify in this section is the underlying decisions you must make to create the needed space for true focus. I believe strongly in order to find your focus, keep it long enough to develop a plan, and then execute the plan; you need to reflect on the following concepts.

1. **Eliminating Distractions and Cutting non-productive things from your life (brutally so)**
2. **Recognizing busy is not the same as productive**
3. **Harnessing the power of Essentialism**
4. **Utilizing batching to free up your time**

We will address each concept in a mini-chapter so you can begin to break down the walls of focus and planning, but before we go there I would like to address a few common myths and concerns that creep up when I talk with people.

The first roadblock people hit is age. I can't be any clearer about this. Your age is not important to this discussion. Alexander the Great conquered most of the known world by his mid-twenties. On the other side of the coin, the oldest person to summit Mount Everest was eighty. It simply doesn't matter when or where you start. Just start. I have taught young students who immediately set the world on fire after graduation because they had a plan and executed correctly.

The second myth that seems to bind people up is a lack of education. I know this is going to sound weird coming from a college professor, but too many people go to college. We have turned college in our country into a holding pen for young people with no idea what they want from life. They are there just to delay being an adult.

There are absolutely professions and dream careers for people that require advanced education. For these people college is a critical and necessary investment of time and resources. For others, it's a total waste of time and money.

If you dream of owning a construction company that rehabs homes, you need to learn how to build things. You don't need to know 17th century English literature. I strongly believe the owner of any business would benefit from taking some college courses in business to learn the fundamentals, but that can happen later and may not result in a full degree.

It is far more important as a society and as parents we work with our young people to determine the best possible path for them in life. If college is the right tool for continuing on the path, then great. If it's not, that's ok too. Your own lack of education is not a drop-dead point for your dreams. In contrast, your advanced education is not a ticket to automatic riches. It's just a tool. Use it appropriately.

The last caution I would give before proceeding is this. Planning is not doing. I realize the title of this section highlights the need to plan and that is true. You do need to take the lay of the land and make plans. However, never mistake those plans for accomplishing anything. When I set out to write this book, I went to great lengths to lay out all the topics I wanted to cover. I reviewed all the source material I wanted to work from. I purchased a software designed to help me organize the structure of the book. I created headers for each chapter and listed what to cover in each. All of that planning amounts to zero until I sit down and actually WRITE the book. At some point planning must become action and execution.

As you review this section and complete the planning guides please keep in mind it won't matter until you do something with it.

DISTRACTED BY DESIGN

Have you ever taken a moment to look around? Do it now. Let it soak in how many things are vying for your attention at this very moment. It's incredible how splintered our attention has become in modern society. Look at this list and try to tell me with a straight face these things aren't impacting your focus in life right now.

- Family
- Friends
- School work
- Job work
- TV
- Your smart phone
- Video games
- Advertising
- The dog
- And finally, the giant time suck known as Social Media

We have reached a point where studies show the majority of people are playing games on their phone while watching TV. We are so distracted that our entertainment needs its own entertainment. There is no possible way you are going to find any room in your head to focus on meaningful work if you can't eliminate some of these obstacles.

Now is the time for me to tell you this will be brutal and painful. You are going to find you need to eliminate things you might actually like. The simple truth remains you have limited time on this planet. You need to get moving on the areas that genuinely matter to you.

The following is a short list of things I suspect are going to fall into the painful cut category.

- Social Media. Just please admit here and now you are addicted. After admitting that, please tell me what actual benefit you are getting from it. Do you feel better afterward? Not likely, since studies show a soaring depression rate among heavy social media users. Are you making new positive connections with possible future clients? No. You are rehashing the same stupid argument with your deadbeat uncle about politics for the 56th time. You are scrolling through someone else's highlight real life and "hate liking" their posts. Would you really be any worse off if you cut this from your life or at least reduced it to a minimum?

- Family. Holy crap. Did this guy just say to cut family from my life? Yes. Yes I did, and I don't apologize for it. In fact, I am sorry no one told you earlier that your family doesn't get to matter simply because they share biology with you. Most family is wonderful and supportive. You have relationships with family you should cherish and nurture. I would be willing to bet you also have a few relatives who are total dipshits. They do nothing but bring you down, criticize your dreams, and generally suck the joy from your life. There is ZERO guilt in cutting them loose and never giving them another thought. You owe them nothing. You owe yourself peace.

- Friends. See all comments from the family section. Good ones stay. Fake ones go.

- Leisure activities. I am all for working less and enjoying life. In fact, I believe strongly AGAINST the 40-hour week. It's arbitrary and has no connection to productivity. That said, reaching your dreams will take work. In the short term that may mean cutting fun stuff so you can focus and get something done. Don't worry though, if you find work you love it won't feel like work anyways.

In order to determine what exactly needs cut from your life, it's imperative to know how you truly spend your time. No need to cut social media if its only 5 minutes a day (see I am not a monster). The next mini chapter will help with this.

SO BUSY YOU FORGOT TO BE PRODUCTIVE

You say you are really busy. So busy you could not imagine making changes and improving your life. You want to work out and get healthy. You want to finish all your schoolwork on time. You want to research that new business opportunity. You want to take that pottery class your friend told you about. If only you had the time to do it all. I call bullcrap. Being "Busy" is a choice.

The truth if you are being honest is you have failed to place priority on the right things in life. However, there is no sense in me arguing with you. First, this is a book and that would be a really one sided and strange argument. Second, I have a better solution. You are going to spend one week tracking everything you do. I mean everything.

This workbook has provided you with a little handy dandy time log. Lawyers are required to track their time for client billing purposes. You are tracking your time for life billing purposes. I have a strong belief that once you evaluate the actual time you "billed" to TV and your iPhone you might feel different.

We are going to start with 30-minute increments. My suggestion for this first round is not to try and alter the schedule out of some weird guilt. Just let your freak flag fly for a week. Well in this case, your distracted and perhaps lazy freak flag. In any case you need to know the truth about how you spend your week.

Couple notes to keep you on track. First, the worksheets in this book would be too small to log 48 entries each day. Plus most people use their phones for everything. So go get one of the cool apps that allows you to track your time each day. Then only use the worksheets at the end to record the results. Second, you do not get to simply list 8 hours everyday for work. The odds are high you did not actually work the whole 8 hours. You surfed the web, chatted with coworkers, played solitaire on the computer and other such activities. Same goes for time at home. Focus on what you are TRULY doing during the day. This is what we are trying to learn.

I find myself to be a very productive and energetic human. In fact, most of the time my wife jokes that I simply can't sit still or relax. Even with this frame of mind I run this exercise on myself every now and then. It's always mind blowing how much time is wasted on things that simply don't matter. Taking time to decompress and relax is important. It will keep you sharp and allow you to stay the course far longer. However, I am not sure two hours a day on social media is productive, relaxing, or decompressing. It's just wasting time. Now it is time for you to break it down (your time that is) and see how much more you can squeeze from this life if you really want to.

HABITS

I think it goes without saying we should try to cut out all those bad habits we have formed over time. How do you know which bad habits I am talking about? Easy. Check your time log. Our time, just like our money, gets focused on things we view as a priority. Not the things we CLAIM are a priority. The actual priorities. Now take a look at your time log. Are there things you spent a whole bunch of time on that make you a little queasy? Did you find yourself constantly doing something that you would prefer not to spend your whole life doing? Those need to go.

The really cool thing about bad habits is you are not limited in the number you are allowed to get rid of. As you go through your list and drill down on your own bad behavior, try to focus on WHY the habit needs to go. Keep asking yourself the true motivation behind dropping this habit. Ultimately it is bad if it's not helping you down the path towards the life you dream of. However, each bad habit can have a life of its own and have other reasons it needs to go. You need to clarify those reasons because they will give you the drive to kick the habit.

HABITS TO GO BYE BYE

Dumb Habit #1

_____

Dumb Habit #2

_____

Dumb Habit #3

***

Now that you have identified your bad habits we are going to break into song and dance. Kidding. That comes later. We are, however, going to look at some important facts around habit development. In order to harness the power of habits you need to truly understand the following concepts:

1. How habits work and are formed
2. How we can redirect our lives to better habits
3. How to create a keystone habit
4. How to use the power of "habit stacking"
5. How to develop your positive habits

Before I begin with your crash course in developing daily habits, I want to give credit where it's due. Much of this info comes from an amazing book called Atomic Habits, by James Clear. For the purpose of this book we are focusing on the key points of his book and incorporating them into an overall life change for you. However, if you are truly interested in digging into the finer points of habits please read his book. It's truly well done.

Now, back to our regularly scheduled programming. Habits of all kinds follow a predictable path. Cue, Craving, Response, Reward. This applies whether it is a positive habit or a negative one. Though it should be noted that habits in isolation are never positive or negative. That label only applies depending on your desired outcome for life. Making a decision to study Spanish 30 minutes each day is only positive if you actually care about learning Spanish. Otherwise the same habit could become a distraction from something you should be doing. In any case you must understand the cycle of habits because this gives you power to change and own them. Let's start with a primer on definitions in the most basic terms:

- Cue - It's the trigger. What begins the process?
- Craving - What does the cue cause you to want?
- Response - How do you satisfy the craving?
- Reward - What's the benefit of responding?

This cycle is repeated over and over until a certain pattern develops. At this point you have created a habit. Well over 99% of these habits happen without any conscious thought from you. Our brains need to have most of life on autopilot so we can focus our true thoughts on important topics at hand.

Take a moment and really think about all the actions in life you take without a second thought to the them. Heck you might not even take a first thought. Don't believe me? Have you ever started driving somewhere on the weekend with your family only to realize you have shifted into autopilot and are headed to work? You accidentally triggered the cue (get in car, head in certain direction) and your mind took over from there. Again, slow down and give some thought to the amount of your life on autopilot.

Now that we have this knowledge, we can break down any negative habits in your life. We simply need to identify which step of the cycle we are going to alter. I personally find the Cue and Response to be the easiest steps to change. If you are struggling to break a habit, take some time to identify what is triggering the process to start and/or how you are responding to the craving.

I have a bad habit of eating late at night when I watch TV. To make it worse, the food is normally sugar heavy crap. In short, I am American. To break this habit, I can approach it from two angles. The first is to identify the Cue. In this case when my butt hits the recliner my brain is triggered to want something else going on. The second is to analyze my response. In my case, I respond by grabbing some food to snack on. It is boredom, not nourishment needs. To break the habit, I have two choices. I could break the Cue by simply not sitting down to watch TV. If I never stop being active until I go to bed, I find I never have the craving. However, this isn't always realistic. I like TV and will sit down at some point. My second choice is to simply change the response system. I could get out of my chair and hop on my exercise ball to do some crunches. If I do this long enough the Cue now triggers a new response. Over time a new habit is formed.

You can apply this concept to any habit you are struggling to break. After you master the art of breaking habits, you can apply the exact same system to creating new positive ones. Decide on strong, clear, obvious Cues. Identify the craving it will trigger, how you will respond, and the reward for doing so. Wake up in the morning (Cue), Desire a clean mouth to kiss spouse (craving), Brush teeth (response), minty breath (reward). Repeat until it's a habit.

* * *

Once you master the art of creating good habits it is time to choose the Keystone Habit. This one specific habit is a critical piece of developing positive momentum. You will read about habit stacking in the next paragraph. For now, just know that it's doing habits back to back to back. In order to begin this process, you need the Keystone. This habit is the master seed that begins everything.

For myself, I start each workday by making a list of to-do items. What gets placed on the list is less important than the act of creating it. I can speak personally to the power of the Keystone habit. When I begin listing my items for the day my brain makes a VERY clear shift into work mode. I lose all distraction and begin the momentum of the process. It carries directly into checking and responding to emails, typing up reports, checking in on my staff, writing a chapter of this book and so on. The one habit I commit to fully each day starts the engine and allows me to flow directly into my other requirements. This brings us to the next point about habits.

Habit stacking is a simple and powerful concept. It allows you to build momentum and knock out a bunch of items in one shot. In the most basic form, you are using the "response" of one habit to be the "cue" for the next.

Take my example. I begin with my keystone habit of making a to-do list for the day. The "response" in this habit is the actual creation of the list. This immediately triggers a cue for me to check my email. Once I am done responding to my emails, it triggers a cue to check on my staff. And so on.

This tool can be used to insert even unpleasant tasks. You say you hate that one stupid report you must create each week. So much so that you put it off until the last minute. Try inserting it into the chain of positive momentum habits. This way it just becomes "what you do" instead of a standalone item you dread.

＊

The final piece I will touch on is the power of writing your habits down and TRACKING them. Whether you are trying to break a habit or develop a new one, you need to write down all 4 parts of the habit. This process will solidify for you what exactly is happening and move the thought process from the unconscious to the conscious mind. By doing this you will gain control over the process. You can't change what you aren't fully aware of. The tracking process keeps the entire endeavor at the front of your mind. This allows you to focus on it. I would keep your new positive habits to no more than 4-5 at a time. Work on them until they become a true routine habit and fade to the back of your mind because they are so automatic. Then repeat the process with new ones. (Side note. I really like the phone app DONE for tracking habits. Super clean and easy to use.)

I have included a worksheet with this book that provides a template for breaking down the 3 bad habits you listed above as well as 3 new ones you would like to form. Be deliberate in filling this template out so you can internalize the steps of the process. By bringing the steps to clarity you can work on changing whichever step necessary for improvement.

168 HOURS OF PURE BLISS

As mentioned earlier, I am not someone who likes to hear people say they are busy. That word literally means nothing. Being busy is just another way of saying you can't plan and prioritize well enough to not overload yourself. My schedule is very full. I work a full-time job, teach at the university, sometimes coach sports, give speeches, and in this case try to write a book. All of these things are my choice. Repeat after me, "Being busy is a CHOICE'. There is no exception to this rule.

When I hear someone complain they can't get to the gym and exercise I simply nod my head and die a little inside. You could absolutely get to the gym. You CHOOSE not to go. How long was that show you watched last night? What time did you get up this morning? It's not true you can't get to the gym. You simply don't place a priority on doing so. That's actually ok. Just own it. Your time log should have shown you how much time you waste in a week. If something is not getting done in your life right now, it's because you don't value it enough. No judgement here. Just facts.

Now is the time to throw a little math at you. Do you know what the number 168 represents? It's the total number of hours in a week. It also happens to be more than enough to build an incredible and balanced life. Try breaking the number down real fast and you will see just how much time is really available to you.

- 7 days x 8 hours of sleep = 56 hours used
- 5 days x 10 hours (8 working, 1 commuting, 1 eating lunch) = 50 hours used

So far you have used 106 hours for your "just too much to do anything else in life" requirements of work and sleep. This leaves 62 hours for other pursuits. Read that again. In a normal week you have 62 hours to dedicate towards a better life. For you those hours may be used for family time, home projects, taking classes, coaching, volunteering, cleaning house or whatever else floats your boat. The point is they are yours.

Also, some real talk to keep us straight. The average American actually works about 35 hours a week. The people who say they work 60-70 hours a week, simply don't. There was a national survey done including time tracking, and it showed those people who claim 60-70 hours actually work less than 50. It's just a part of our culture to claim excessive working hours. We believe it makes us a hero or something. The truth is all hours beyond a certain level (different by person and profession) are simply not effective. We burn out and our production plummets. So those extra hours are not worth investing in the same thing the first 50 were.

Returning to our original idea of 62 hours left. This assumes a 40-hour work week. This is totally arbitrary. In our new, mostly knowledge work driven society, there is no logic behind 40 hours. If you work from home, you also eliminate the commute. You could comfortably shave another 10-15 hours from the total and still maintain positive professional results. This could drive your available time up into the 70 hours range each week. This is 10 hours PER DAY on average.

This is why I highlight that being busy is not the same thing as being productive. Being busy simply means moving around a lot. Being productive means establishing priorities and working specifically towards them. College students are notorious for saying, "I'm so busy". Which, frankly, as parents who work, take care of a family, and generally handle everything we laugh at these comments. In any case, it's also nonsense. I immediately ask them what they did the three previous nights. I know from experience the odds of them coming out of this question clean are very low. Somewhere in their routine over the past few days will be copious amounts of wasted time. I tell them if you dream of being an author, then what are you writing TODAY. If you want to be a finance manager, what formula are you mastering TODAY? If you aim to start your own business, what connections are you making TODAY?

The whole point of the time log exercise was to highlight that you are not in fact "busy". You might be disorganized and lack priorities in life, but you are rarely too busy to accomplish things you care about. Try being productive for a few days. Pare your schedule down to things you truly care about and do only those things. Then tell me how "busy" you are.

KEEP THE ESSENTIAL THINGS ESSENTIAL

There has a been a huge rush in popular culture over the past few years towards minimalism. This is the idea of removing as much clutter from your life as possible. Less clothes, smaller house, digitizing documents, and in general just having "less". I support this concept. Our culture for the past 50 years has driven a hoarding mentality. We buy things just to buy them. We own houses that are too large and still we rent storage facilities. This is crazy sauce to me. So please, research and take part in the minimalism movement. It's good for your budget and good for the planet. This, however, is not the aim of this chapter.

Essentialism is a close relative of minimalism. The difference is Essentialism doesn't, by definition, look to reduce anything. Instead it aims for "the right stuff". In every facet of your life there are key drivers. Most people have heard of the 80/20 rule. It states that 80% of your returns come from 20% of your investments. This principle applies across a vast spectrum of your life. 20% of the things you do with your kids like vacations, holidays, zoo trips etc. will generate 80% of their childhood memories. 20% of the clients you call and obtain will generate 80% of your sales. With this idea in mind you must focus hard on the 20%.

Sometimes an example helps clarify the concept. Let's say you are considering opening a pizza shop. You know there are hundreds of things you must consider and plan for to make this happen. You must pick a building, hire employees, find vendors, get insurance, pick a name, create pricing and so on. The number of things needed to start a business can seem overwhelming. However, none of these things matter if your pizza doesn't taste amazing. The quality of your pizza is ESSENTIAL to the business. There is little benefit to working on all the other multitude of items required if no one likes your pizza. You must get that correct first. There is not a single career, job, project, or life choice that is not impacted in a similar manner.

Every area of your life can have essentialism applied to it. If you feel limited in your time and resources than you must narrow your focus to those items and activities essential to making the whole thing go. Marriages take a ton of work and compromise. However, if your spouse knows beyond a doubt that you love them and have their best interest at heart, the rest can be worked out. Therefore, you should focus on that ESSENTIAL trait. You can spend hours putting together a Powerpoint, but if the audience doesn't care about the topic then it's meaningless. I tell my students to carefully study the syllabus for every class. If they have 7 projects all worth 5 points each, and 1 test worth 100 points then it should be clear where the focus needs to be. A critical skill I ask my students to develop as they move from the Convergence Point into Unleashed is the ability to clearly identify the essential element of any task or project. Every single thing you face in this life, whether it's having children or starting a business, works from this principle. A very small number of actions have a critical impact. You must learn to deliver on those key markers.

BATCH YOUR WAY TO FREEDOM

Can I share a secret with you? There is no such thing as multitasking for humans. I know, I know. You have been told for years that it represents the ultimate job skill. You can be a valuable employee by being able to do 32 things at once. The only small problem with this theory is, it's not possible. Not just for you, but anyone. Our brains don't work that way. The Harvard Business Review did a research project which has since been repeated by many others in which they tested a person's ability to "multitask". The conclusion was not how effective certain people could be. It was simply that it's not possible at all.

We are able to process multiple "tasks" in the background of our subconscious brain for sure. You can literally walk and chew gum at the same time. However, you cannot review email and respond while also actively participating on the conference call. Your brain can only focus on one primary active task at a time. In fact, by trying to "multitask", you actually splinter your focus entirely and slow down both processes. There is a cost to this way of working known as switching costs. These costs are the lost time needed for your brain to shut down one train of thought and redirect to another task. Think about when you stop reading that email and try to refocus on the question your boss just asked you. There is a short time where you are stuck in the middle and that delay is the switching cost. When you do this over and over each day you lose huge volumes of time to the abyss.

So how do you complete multiple tasks through a day? To be clear, I am not naive enough to believe you will not face interruptions. Those are part of being in the professional world. I am more concerned with how you structure your day to complete multiple tasks without splintering your focus everywhere. The key is a process called "batching". If you can learn this skill, you will find yourself far more valuable to an employer. In fact, it might even make your interview far more interesting when you present a skill no one else has.

Batching in its most simple form is placing tasks into defined time buckets. For example, you may decide you are ONLY checking emails at 10am and 2pm. You will respond to all emails during those windows and knock them all out in one shot. This allows you to completely focus on the task and finish it. Once you are done checking emails, you TURN OFF THE NOTIFICATIONS. This is part of what I critically refer to as structuring your day. We are so conditioned to being notified at every possible moment that we allow infinite distractions. Confess the truth now. When you see the little mail icon pop up on your screen there is a part of you that can't resist the desire to read it. Bingo, you are distracted and possibly dragged down a rabbit hole. The task you were focused on is now forgotten. Time is wasted switching to email mode and then when you finish feeding your addiction you lose time trying to remember where you were and get back into the flow of the project. Only to be distracted moments later by another email. Break the cycle.

Batching can assist to free time in a number of areas. Many American's use a common batching technique without even recognizing it. We only buy groceries once a week instead of at each meal. It's more efficient. You don't need to balance your checkbook and pay bills as they come in. Do it once a week in a large batch. Don't waste time on short conference calls every day. Schedule a large time block on Friday and knock all calls out in one rush. Instead of making eggs every morning, hard boil 30 on Sunday and enjoy all week.

There are limitless options for this technique. Essentially, for anything you find in your life where you are doing small repetitive tasks, you should batch them. Give these tasks a dedicated time block and stop allowing them to distract you all the time. (Author's helpful note. Turn off ALL notifications on your phone and watch with one chosen exception for emergencies. You aren't the POTUS and nothing is that important.)

Chapter 14
The Great Unveiling

"I have not failed. I've just found 10,000 ways that won't work."

-Thomas Edison

There is one major hurdle everyone going through this process struggles with. Telling others you are ready to follow a different path. Reasons for this can be many. For some people, they are afraid of failing after being vocal about change. Others are afraid the world will actively work against their desire to break out. Still others have been shamed into silence by past failures. Whatever the struggle, it can be difficult to pronounce to the world you are trying something different. You no longer accept the path laid before you and want to go your own way. While this step can be scary and uncomfortable, it is also critically important. Let's run through the process of unveiling your new plans to the world.

TIME TO GET CRAZY

The first key thing to wrestle with is when to tell everyone. I have candidly struggled with this my whole life. I have a tendency to share my crazy thoughts very early in the process. For me, it works as a great feedback mechanism. I value seeing other people's reactions and being able to pick their brain for unique ideas. However, this can be seen from outsiders as me bouncing from idea to idea with no focus. It becomes a conundrum. I need feedback, but don't want to be known as crazy. In releasing my ideas too early I run the risk of people not taking them seriously because there is no substance behind them. People won't invest their mental energy on an idea they don't believe has any shot of moving forward. It can't be seen as the flavor of the week.

The other end of the spectrum is also dangerous. Far too many people wait too long in introducing their plans. In doing so, they have gone so far down the path there is little space for changing directions, altering approach, or even taking people's advice on improvement. When your idea is so fleshed out you don't appear interested in changing anything, people simply won't give feedback. They won't want to hurt your feelings, and don't believe it's beneficial anyways since you aren't going to alter course.

All of this leaves us looking for the sweet spot in the middle of this time continuum. You want your plan to take shape, show development, and prove substance without appearing set in stone. You are looking for people to be excited for you and about the idea while still seeing the benefit in helping you. However, you want to have done enough work on your own to ensure the original idea remains strong and your personal vision is not compromised. Remember you want people's advice and guidance, not their opinion on your life.

Once you have established the right time to unveil your plans, you need to focus on how to do it and to whom. These parts will vary depending on your specific path. In any case there will be some key concepts to remember. Let's dive in.

I LIKE YOU, HERE'S MY CRAZY IDEA

We will start with WHOM to tell. To start, it's pretty simple. Only tell people initially you believe will be supportive. There is a strong likelihood your ideas are too young and underdeveloped to withstand heavy criticism or negativity. If you are fresh to the "doing my own thing" club, you will find it difficult to stand strong when the negative Nancy's start chiming in. Sadly, there will always be people in this world who are not happy with just being miserable themselves. They only thrive when they can also ruin other people's lives. They are the absolute worst and people to avoid at all costs early in the process. The person or people you choose to introduce your ideas to can vary largely based on your experience, but I believe some large categories make sense.

Best Friends - *This seems pretty obvious. I have heard ideas from my friends I thought were borderline nuts. I decided, however, to help them anyways because I cared about their success. I truly want my friends to be a success. If a few kind words from me can help on that path, then easy choice. I am quite sure you have at least one friend who will smile and support you even if they believe you are sipping crazy juice. This is ok for the very beginning of the process as you build momentum.*

Mentors - *The title this person holds could vary widely. It could be a professor you have a good connection with. Maybe it's a former boss you worked well with. Maybe there is an elder in your church or club you admire who would be willing to give advice. These people are valuable because they know you well enough to be committed, without being so emotionally connected they are willing to support you no* *matter what. Mentors can provide honest and insightful feedback, while remaining firmly in your corner. Since there is no benefit in the outcome for them, the mentor can stand at arm's length and provide perspective to the whole process.*

You will take notice as to the major group I did NOT mention. Family. They can be challenging people to support your dreams in the early stages. They are often so invested in your life they will struggle to maintain objectivity. If we are talking parents, they will have their own dreams for your life that may not jive with your new path. Siblings have their own priorities. Grandparents may have different value systems entirely. There will also be a component of the known that is hard to overcome. Family has watched you grow for so long they will struggle to reconcile an intentional choice to be different. Any advice they try to give will be colored by their history and perspective of you. I am not asking you to go it alone on this path to a better place and leave your family behind. I am simply cautioning against them being early adopters of the program.

Once you have gathered your initial supporters and taken time to incorporate their thoughts, it's time for phase two. This is the painful step. You need to approach the people you know are going to tear into your plan. It's nice to believe everyone will be supportive and your life will be rosy moving forward. It simply doesn't work that way. The harsh truth is you shouldn't want it to work that way. You need some negative feedback. You need to be challenged. There is an absolute certainty you have missed things in your exuberance. You need people who will point out flaws in your plan. People who will question your ability to execute or stay committed. Frankly, people who simply don't believe in you.

You prove nothing in convincing people who already support you. Only by breaking through the challenges presented by the naysayers can you truly know you are moving in the right direction. Whether people are giving you harsh advice out of love or simple negativity doesn't actually matter. All criticisms must be addressed in the end. Therefore, all criticisms have some value.

If your chosen path starts to crumble under the pressure of true scrutiny, who is to blame? The people pointing out your flaws, or your poorly developed plan? It's acceptable to admit you were wrong, as long as you have a plan to fix it moving forward. Fail and then fail better.

TAILOR YOUR SUITS.....AND YOUR MESSAGE

If you have determined the right mix of people to begin unveiling your plan to, then you need to give thought as to the best way to approach them. There is no one right answer to this question. It will depend greatly on who the person is, their personality, your relationship, and the response you are hoping for. However, there will always be key ideas to keep in mind as you prepare your unveiling to various people.

***

The first question you must ask yourself before you tell someone about your plan is, "what do I want from this individual"? There is no chance you are looking for the same response from a professor as you are from your mom. Each person you encounter during your journey serves a different role. You need to be aware of the role you want them to play. Your best friend is likely being asked to serve as nothing more than head cheerleader. You need that person to be your personal hype machine. Your hype man doesn't need to know the nuts and bolts of how you plan to pull this magic trick off. They only need to know you are awesome and the world must bow to your amazing-ness. Your college professor on the other hand is not interested in your raw coolness. You simply need that person to give advice on how to execute certain pieces of the plan. All of this is completely normal. Every team has various members with different roles.

You should give thought to which role each person in your life will play. Tailor your message. When I discuss this book with people in my sphere, I must be careful with how it is presented initially. When I speak to my students about it, I can give more details because it impacts them directly and there is a presumed expertise on my part. (Side note, they haven't figured out yet I am an idiot.) When I present it to a few people who are also writers, I focus on the process and how to go about getting my message out. I am leaning on their industry specific knowledge. For my friends and colleagues, I merely hand them a draft and wait for a reaction.

I need to see and feel how they react to the book. When I mention the book to my family, I gloss over everything because they already believe me an idiot and assume this is another wild goose chase. I will simply ask them to read it when it's done. You will find yourself in the constant position of deciding how to provide information to each person you meet. Again, be clear on what you need from them and then tailor the message.

The second question to ask is, "how would the information comes across best to this person"? Again, no two people are going to be the same. If you want me to review your financial statements, I actually need to see an Excel file with numbers on it. Maybe go all out and create a fancy PowerPoint with charts and stuff. However, if you bust out the PowerPoint tonight at the bar with your buddies, things could get awkward really quickly. This book is designed to help you focus on your better life moving forward. It is not a business startup book. There may be no need to develop a written plan. Or there might be. Some people in your life will jump on board and support you better if they see an actual well thought out written plan. Other people in your life want to hear the story of tomorrow straight from you. It will not be enough to know what you want to say to everyone around. You also need to know HOW you will say it.

As you work through this step it may be helpful to return to your Mission Statement from way back in the early chapters. No matter what you plan to say, who you plan to say it to, or how you plan to say it, your message must be clear and concise. It must speak directly to the heart of the change you are trying to make in your life.

Chapter 15
Educate yourself

*"Education is the most powerful weapon which you can use
to change the world."*
-Nelson Mandela

So far in this book you have been down a path of being educated ABOUT yourself. Now you need to focus on educating yourself on a topic. You need to gain skills and knowledge that will allow you to rise through the ranks of your chosen career path. Regardless of the field you choose to pursue, there will be more information to learn than time in your life. There will be foundational skills and knowledge that could take years to master. Next comes the more subtle expert level material. At some point, your knowledge is augmented by your experience working in the field.

There is a well-known concept that it requires 10,000 hours to become a master of something. To place that in perspective, it would require 3 hours of practice every single day for 10 years to reach mastery. This can seem daunting, but society only truly rewards the masters. Whatever the circumstance you must always be learning and educating yourself on things that matter to your career. This, however, can be trickier than it seems. We have a few branches of this tree we need to explore together.

JACK OF MANY TRADES

There are very few careers that will work by mastering only one specific skill. Even those careers that do are not rewarding or high paying. The simplicity, by definition, means anyone can do it. This drives the value down. Instead you are going to focus on careers that are complex and multi-layered. This can work both against you and for you. The downside is most successful careers take time because you are trying to gain expertise on multiple fronts. This can be offset though by your ability to achieve small successes more often. You spend time going to law school and studying to be a lawyer. This is a grueling and long process. At the same time, you are taking short communications classes to be more effective working with future clients. You also work with a consultant on branding and marketing so you can build a solid reputation.

Many of these ancillary skills can be learned in a shorter time but give you momentum to stay the course on the longer game. It is critically important to research your chosen path and determine ALL the skills it will take to be truly successful. The major you happen to study in college is but a small piece of the puzzle. By learning the true breadth of the skills you need to master, you give yourself the opportunity for positive momentum and small victories along the way.

NO NEWS IS GOOD NEWS

An interesting paradox of educating yourself is that it is very possible to know too much. More correctly, it's possible to seek to know too much. It is an almost certainty you need to learn a huge volume of information to be truly great in your chosen field. Therefore, you need to go on an information diet about everything else.

Stop watching the news. There is nothing useful being presented. Honestly, when was the last time something was discussed on the nightly news, in a newspaper, or on a talking head show that truly mattered to your life? My guess is never. As a society we have been conditioned to believe we need to be informed about everything going on in our world.

This simply isn't true. Almost every data point and piece of information you will come across is useless to you. Your focus needs to be on receiving information from sources that truly represent opportunities for you to learn material about your chosen field.

Now, to be clear I am not asking you to be an ignorant member of society. Of course, there can value in remaining informed about important topics happening around you. There will be items on the ballot when you go to vote that you should understand. Elections are better when voters actually know something about candidates. Buying a new car without any research is a bad idea. However, none of the above examples means you personally must do any of the information seeking.

have a very good friend who is obsessed with politics. After many late-night discussions I know the way he thinks, and we are closely aligned politically. Before elections I call him and ask him to give me the 10-minute short version of who and what I should vote for. I don't watch the debates, pay attention to commercials, spend hours researching the zoning laws or do any other such time wasting. If you need to buy a car you can call my 12-year-old son and in 10 minutes he will identify the perfect car for you. He knows everything there is to know about cars. Honestly, I maybe see a career for him in the future based on his passion for cars. In any case, you need to go on the information diet and stop caring so much about all the useless data out there.

BEING TOO MUCH OF A SMARTASS

The last paradox of educating yourself is knowing the wrong things or knowing things at the wrong level. I will be the very first to admit I am not the best "finance" person in my department at the university. My knowledge level is below that of all my colleagues. However, I am asked to teach the entry level classes in finance, and my knowledge is more than sufficient to accomplish the task. I would see very marginal improvements in my job performance by increasing my finance knowledge from say 85 to 92 on a 100 scale, if teaching the class only requires a level 75 knowledge. Instead I have chosen to increase my skills and knowledge in other areas closely tied to my classroom performance. I work hard to improve my verbal communications, study learning style theory, develop better case study models and so forth. Ultimately my positive reviews from students are more driven by an ability to distill tough topics into small digestible chunks than they are by being level 100 smart in finance. Put another way. If a teacher knows 100 out of 100, but can only communicate and transmit 65 to the students, and I know 90 out of 100 but can transmit all 90, who is the better teacher?

Ultimately, you will benefit from continuing to increase your foundational knowledge within your chosen field. I in no way want to discourage mastering your field to level 100. In fact, I fully support this process. I only caution that your career and ultimately your life path will require many skills that are not taught through normal schooling in a traditional sense. You must educate yourself fully on the skills that will matter most to your path. You will know you are heading down the right path of education and learning when you begin making connections that would not seem obvious to the beginner.

Chapter 16
Live by choices

"Do not go where the path may lead, go instead where there is no path and leave a trail."
-Ralph Waldo Emerson

The final piece to making the leap from dreamer to doer (Convergence to Unleashed) is simply choices. No matter how much information I provide through this book, it is still a choice on your part to act.

IT IS CRITICALLY IMPORTANT YOU OWN THE FACT THAT EVERY SINGLE THING IN YOUR LIFE IS A RESULT OF THE CHOICES YOU HAVE MADE. YOU MUST LIVE WITH THOSE CHOICES. PERIOD. NO EXCEPTIONS.

In order to ensure the best possible odds of a positive outcome from moving into action mode let's focus on 4 drivers for your choices.

- **Attention and Intention**
- **Have a bias towards action**
- **Constant steps forward**
- **Focus on micro-decisions**

GIVE ATTENTION TO YOUR INTENTION

When you set out to live by your choices, it makes sense to target those choices on things you care about. This is where attention and intention come into play. You need to place Attention on the things in your life that truly matter. Your priorities are not determined by the things you say. They are determined by the way you spend your time. The things you care about get your attention. It's really that simple. You need to ensure your attention is being given to the highest priorities you are claiming for your life.

If you want to start your own business, but spend 10 minutes a week on it, can you really call it a priority? The key to shifting that paradigm is Intention. You must determine where your attention will go based on Intention. Your choices can not be by accident or happenstance. You cannot luck your way into a successful career. There is no such thing as luck. Lazy people believe in luck. Focused people believe in making intentional choices to place themselves in the best place to take advantage of an opportunity.

At the core of this topic is taking a short moment every time you are presented with options to decide where your *attention* should be and then *intentionally* choosing the best path. Never allow things to just "happen" in your life.

A CALL TO ARMS

The worst enemy of most people's dreams is paralysis by analysis. We simply over think everything. We become obsessed with making sure we have every last detail worked out before we are willing to take any action. Planning has benefits. This is not in question. Failing to do any planning is a recipe for disaster. However, creating a plan is not actually DOING anything. Only in taking action are you moving forward.

I spent some time before writing this book laying out the chapters and general road we would follow. I would be lying though if I claimed to have it thoroughly detailed out. I reached a point where I needed to have a bias towards action. I needed to simply start writing. A book has never resulted from planning chapters. It results from WRITING chapters.

This critical concept must become a part of your DNA. Please take time to plan your path forward, but when the time comes you must ACT. No more planning. No more rethinking the strategy. You will regret far more things you did not do in life than the things you did do. If you fail the first go around, then fail better next time. In any case, you only move forward towards the life you are dreaming of by actually moving forward. The bias towards action can provide multiple benefits.

- You gain momentum by truly accomplishing something. Even 5 minutes spent writing my book brought me closer to completing it than 1 hour planning another chapter.

- You begin gathering additional data points to improve on later. Much of your planning time is spent trying to eliminate all possible negative outcomes. You are trying to predict how certain actions will play out. Guess what? If you simply do the action you will know for certain and can move forward accordingly.

- Lastly, your bias to action will begin breaking down the wall of fear. If you are honest with yourself, you have failed to launch because you are scared. Once you decide to make even a small move forward you will realize the fear was misplaced. In almost every circumstance, the thing you imagined being awful was at worst mildly unpleasant. You will begin to realize you can be bolder, and the negative setbacks are not truly that bad.

JUST REPEAT AFTER ME....LEFT FOOT. RIGHT FOOT. REPEAT

Following closely on the heels of bias to action is ensuring constant steps forward. It doesn't matter the size of the step. Simply move forward. In almost every situation the process becomes more than the goal. As you look to the future and determine your final desired outcome, you will realize there are a hundred things to accomplish along the way.

If you remember back a few chapters, the focus should be on the essential items most of the time. These are the choices and decisions with the largest impact on the final outcome. However, every step must be taken at some point no matter how small. By keeping this perspective, you will be able to celebrate the small victories and stay the course.

Make it a mindset that every day I will choose to act and choose to accomplish one small step down the path. Constantly moving forward has the power to confirm your purpose to yourself and others. It becomes really tough to argue you won't make it to your chosen destination if you are moving closer every day. Focus on these small steps forward and celebrate them. They matter more than you realize.

MICRO-DECISIONS, MASSIVE IMPACT

The final piece to living by choices is realizing how small the key choices can truly be. Every major decision and every fork in the road started with a micro-decision early on. This is the case for every single choice you will make in your life. For this reason, it is important to focus on any choices that have larger ripple effects. You should spend time concentrating to make a positive decision on the critical choices that appear each day.

Let's say you claim to have made a choice to lose weight. That choice doesn't matter at all if the next time you head into the kitchen you come back with chocolate instead of an apple. It is the tiny choice between two foods that determine if the larger goal is met.

How about if you make a "decision" to have better oral health? Well, first that isn't a decision. That is a goal. For many people meeting this goal would mean going to the dentist twice a year. Yes that is important, but the true *decisions* are the tiny ones you will need to make along the way. You must choose sugar free gum when you are standing in the grocery lane. You must choose to floss daily when you are tired and want to go to bed. You must not skimp on brushing time twice each day. All of these tiny repetitive choices are the true drivers behind whether that visit to the dentist will be pleasant or not. *(side note: this was a shameless plug to make my wife happy since she works at a dental office)*

Keep a clear focus on minute by minutes choices and whether they directly promote the ultimate goals you have set for yourself. These micro-decisions build on each other to become the foundation of the larger plan you are creating for yourself.

Part V:

LEGENDARY

We have now reached the point in our journey where you are a wild success in life. People envy the awesome that you are. Ok, maybe it's not exactly that amazing just yet. However, you have traveled far enough down the path that you are fairly certain success is on the horizon. You possess a newfound inner confidence and know your own voice. You have discovered the calling on your life and know the career that can fulfill your soul. You have also taken steps to launch out on your own and live the life you only dreamed of before. All of this is fantastic.

Yet, there is still a whole life in front of you. There is still time to do amazing things and impact others. There is time to branch out and explore the ever-changing landscape of your world.

If I am honest with you, this is the phase of life I find myself in. I write this section fully aware that it still applies in every way to my life. I am not a finished product, nor will I ever be. Therefore, this section of the book is written as a guide for both you and me. It is a short section and never truly ends. You and I will remain in the loop of self-reflection and improvement until the ride ends. So let's take a look together at the process we can use to ensure we get the most out of the crazy, amazing life we have built for ourselves.

Chapter 17
Balance in all things

"The only true wisdom is in knowing you know nothing."
-Socrates

We all need to take some mental yoga classes and find balance. This is never more important than when you have finally "arrived". You have spent time finding your true voice, identifying and securing that amazing career that satisfies your soul, and making your dreams come alive. It all seems to be going incredibly well for you. So what's next? The answer is to think more like a stool. Wait, what did he just say? I said stool. You heard me. Though I concede that may need some explanation.

Every good stool has three legs. If it didn't it would fall over. Stools with two legs are called, well broken, and those are hard as hell to sit on. In the case of your life there are also three legs you need to take care of to ensure good balance. Your health, career, and relationships. The cold truth is you only have so much time and energy to dedicate to this life. Every moment you remained focused on one of the three areas is, by definition, time removed from the other two. There is no compromise here. In order to ensure you can truly maintain a slow consistent burn over many years you will need to balance and nurture all three areas.

You must learn to identify the critical few over the trivial many. In a twist of irony, the more successful you become the more demands there will be on your time. It's a simple law of attraction. People like to be around successful people. They will also want to place demands on your time. There will be more opportunities (the trivial many) than you care to participate in. You should remain focused on the core things (the critical few) which bring you true joy and happiness. There is nothing wrong with living a life focused on less, but better. Let us take a moment to address the three legs of our mighty stool.

HEALTHY...THEN WEALTHY AND WISE

Did you know you are going to die? I apologize, if that was news to you. I hope it wasn't a spoiler on this movie of your life. However, that doesn't mean you should ignore your health along the way. The only possible way to achieve all your goals in this life is to remain healthy enough to accomplish them. Your health is a critical component to long term success. It also turns out, your family prefers you, well alive. It does no one any good if you literally kill yourself working ninety hours a week to accomplish your dream, only to crash three hours after succeeding. Your health is a critical part of this whole process. I won't bore you with lectures on your diet, and what fitness routine you should be following. There are roughly fourteen million books on these topics. (author's note, I am rounding to the nearest 14 million).

What I want to highlight as we focus on balance is the importance of your health overall. Therefore, even within the health topic of this book you need balance. You should have a positive workout routine that energizes you and makes you feel stronger. You should have a nutrition program that supports your lifestyle and makes you feel good inside. You should explore and discover some form of meditation, mindfulness or other brain space technique. Lastly, buy an awesome mattress and get some freaking sleep.

Think of it this way. Your health is a weapon you can use towards achieving your goals. Less doctor appointments means more time to focus on work. Better physical fitness means more quality time spent with your children outside throwing the ball. Better sleep means you aren't a grump ass every day and people might actually want to be around you.

YOUR JOB IS TO BALANCE

Your career also requires some balance as you expand your influence. If you followed the path of this book and targeted the perfect profession, there is a good chance you exploded into success. You spent a large chunk of time crafting the perfect career and finding rewards along the way. At a certain point, however, even you career needs to branch out. You can't stagnate in your comfort area. How do we take a career built around growth and find balance? Well, we need to view our career in three pieces.

First, you must take steps to automate and reduce the bulk of your tasks that are currently consuming your day. You have likely spent a large amount of time mastering pieces of your job. This is how you got to your current heights. However, this doesn't mean you must do those same things forever to no end. It's ok to offload even the items you have come to master. If you take some time to review your workday, it is likely you will find opportunities to streamline the mundane and free up time. Your existing work must be strengthened to a point where it can survive without you for a bit.

Second, we need to look for the chances to grow the mastery we have developed. Our career will change and morph over time. There will be moments when our current mastery can open new chances for us to grow. This is an opportunity for you to personally expand without the fear and anxiety that comes from the initial jump we discussed a few chapters ago.

The final step to balance your career is to explore entirely new universes. Do you remember the rush you had way back when you first leaped into a new life path? The moments of equal part anxiousness and giddiness. You need those to pop back up every now and then. Those are the moments we really grow by leaps and bounds. It is important to maintain a little bit of edge throughout our entire career. The excitement mixed with fear of failure will keep us sharp over time. Feed off that and seek it out from time to time. It will give balance to the mundane areas you have already mastered.

IN THE END IT'S ALL ABOUT PEOPLE

The final piece of balance in life is your relationships. For many hard drivers this is the toughest area to get right. I know personally it can be difficult to place enough focus on the close relationships in my life. I spend so much time trying to help students and coworkers, I forget about the people who need me at home. However, this concept of balanced relationships isn't just about spending more time with family. Your life involves far too many relationships to boil down to something this simple. You need to have friends in your life. You need to have mentors. You need to have enemies (well at least frennemies). You need professional peers. All the different types of relationships in your life are valuable and deserve some time and energy put into growing them. The balance piece is determining how much time and energy each one deserves. This is a tough ask, and one many people (myself included) rarely get right for long stretches of time.

You have a life that is already split into career, personal health, and relationships. Now you must take that one chunk and break it down even farther. This is why often family and friends feel they are getting shortchanged on the time spectrum. The key for you to remember is the balance must meet YOUR intended purpose for life. This could require some changes to your definitions and how you think about things. If you have a life goal to change lives of others, perhaps you should consider time spent with your children as part of your professional life. You are certainly changing their life. Perhaps you can double dip on time by working out with your best friend each day.

In any case it is important to take a step back and evaluate all the types of relationships you have developed over time. Which ones are important and need further fertilizing, and which may have served their purpose and can now be scaled back?

Ultimately the idea of balance is finding a sweet spot. I know I have broken your life into three clean parts. The truth we all know is life doesn't work nearly this cleanly. The areas bleed into one another. Time gets mashed up as you try to respond to a work email while playing a board game with your family. You get pulled from a critical work meeting because a child is sick at school. Your workout is interrupted by a friend's frantic emergency. Accepting the reality of this jumbled schedule is fine. The critical concept to grasp onto is that each area DOES need attention. Each area does need its own space. In order to find the true balance, you must hold fast to your concrete priorities and ensure you are committing the time to make each grow.

It is equally important that you remind everyone in your sphere that in order for you to be whole, you must be allowed to give some space in your life to all three areas.

Chapter 18
Uplift

"As we express our gratitude, we must never forget that the highest appreciation is not to utter words, but to live by them."
-John F. Kennedy

I have asked much of you in this book with regards to reflection and self-discovery. I have forced you to face some ugly truths about yourself and your past. In fact, it would be a strange self-improvement book if it didn't focus mostly on you. However, this is my one opportunity to ask you to break away from your own interests for a moment.

There is nothing more important in the journey towards an incredible life lived than the chance to bring others with you. You not only have a responsibility to the world to be your best self, but also to assist others in the doing the same. Candidly, it's the reason I was driven to write this book. If even one person alters course and finds a better path for life, the effort put into this book will have been worth it. You don't get to be the exception. **You owe the people around you the effort it takes to lift them up**. You cannot live a life truly fulfilled if you live in isolation. If you spend all your time celebrating your own success without helping others to find that path, you will be left feeling empty. So how do you go about bringing others along for the ride to the top? I am so glad you asked.

I find there are multiple ways to assist the people in your circle of influence. Which alternative you choose will largely depend on your skill set and your time constraints. Each method below can have a tremendous impact so please do not feel they are all required. Each has its place, and like everything else we have discussed you are likely more talented and drawn to specific ones. In general, I believe you can uplift those around you by:

- **Mentoring**
- **Volunteering**
- **Educating**
- **Donating**

MENTORS MATTER

Let's begin with the most personal and intense version of uplifting others. Mentoring. For hundreds of generations the idea of mentoring was expected of all great professionals. This was the primary vehicle for passing down knowledge and wisdom to the next generation. Once public schools became the norm, however, we moved away from this type of relationship. That is a travesty. The direct mentoring relationship is powerful far beyond anything a school could hope to achieve.

If you have the time, expertise, and willingness to work directly with another person in bringing them alive and helping them grow, you should absolutely do so. The benefits are immense. There is no greater gift you can give a single person than your time and energy directly committed to their success. There are also amazing benefits to you as the mentor. You will be able to see and feel the impact you are having in a very direct way. This will keep you motivated and committed to the process better than simply donating money to a cause. It will also give you the opportunity to learn a tremendous amount about yourself. As your mentee grows and expands, you will experience the journey with them. This is the most concrete way to know you have left the world a better place than you found it. Ultimately this feeling is similar to the joy parents find in watching their children grow to be successful. It is not about taking credit for their success, but rather pride in knowing the good you do is being multiplied out by another.

Consider finding an organization that specializes in this area. It will provide you with resources and support to ensure you are "doing it right" as it were.

VOLUNTEERS ALWAYS NEEDED

The second way to bring light to others is through good old fashion volunteering. There are so many options for doing this in your community that a whole book could be written on just this topic. In fact, my guess is hundreds of them have been. Volunteering can be incredibly powerful as an investment of your time. For someone like yourself who has grown into an incredibly successful person, time is a precious resource. In this book, you have taken multiple steps to identify just what your time is worth and what you should be spending it on. If you now choose to set aside some of that time for your community and those that need you, it sends an incredibly powerful message. You are telling people how much they matter and how committed you are to them by breaking from your high earning time to assist them.

The opportunity to volunteer is also an incredible means for you to remember this life is not always about what you need. As I have mentioned before, and will mention again, you owe this world a debt for everything you have. It is **OUR RESPONSIBILITY** to bring others up with us. Not one person gets to be above the obligation to assist their community. Find a cause you believe in, and then commit your most precious resource of time to it.

TEACH THEM TO FISH

Education is clearly near and dear to my heart. I was born to teach, so this obligation comes easy to me. However, I want to be clear about this topic. This is not only about teaching in a formal setting. That is called a job. Yes, I am a paid college professor. True statement. It is hard to take credit for the job you get paid to do. In my case though I am always teaching. I can't turn it off. Almost every conversation I have with people becomes a lesson. I feel a tremendous responsibility to pass knowledge to others where I believe it can help them. I get a rush from it.

There are so many areas of life where more people would benefit from increased expertise and knowledge. My guess is you know one of these areas very well. It is likely what you built your incredible life on. If this is true, then you should give serious thought to educating others in what you know. There can be endless means to do this. There are churches hosting classes, clubs doing lecture series, schools asking for volunteers, and even people you meet on the street seeking information they may not even know they need. The list of chances to educate someone in an area you know well could go on forever.

The incredible power of education for me is the multiplying effect it has. When I work with a young couple to educate them on personal finance, there is a high chance their children will learn it from them in the future. My one act of educating someone has the power to filter down through families and impact far more than just the person I talked to initially.

I am absolutely biased in this discussion, but I believe education is the single most powerful tool we have for uplifting our communities. The multiplying effect has no limits. Therefore, if you are truly knowledgeable in a given area please consider joining the ranks of teachers, even if informally. You could impact untold lives you may never even know about.

MONEY IS A TOOL, USE IT WISELY

The final option I will bring to the table for uplifting your community is donating. It may sound crass, but there will always be incredibly positive programs in your community that simply need funding to move forward.

During your beginning stages of building an awesome life, you may lack time to volunteer, may not yet be comfortable enough in your knowledge base to become a teacher, and may not have the opportunity to mentor. However, you can still provide funding to allow others to do the work that needs done. This is perfectly acceptable, and you should feel no shame in doing so. In fact, there is an argument to be made that the super high wage earners among us should actually focus on this type of uplifting. Not everyone has the ability to earn really high incomes. If you do, it's possible the best use of your time from the community's perspective is for you to go earn the money and then pass some of it along.

I would only caution that if you find yourself in this situation, you remember that part of uplifting the community is becoming connected to it. I would urge you not to simply become the banker. This could leave you feeling empty and perhaps not sensing the true impact you can have. Ultimately this whole process is about people first. Money is nice as a tool. It is never the goal.

Whichever option you choose to pursue, always keep in mind you made it where you are with help from others. Even the most independent and stubborn person requires the assistance of others as they rise. This directly means that you owe much of your success to others along the way. This in turn means you owe it to others to carry on this tradition.

Chapter 19
Reflect

"Being entirely honest with oneself is a good exercise."
-Sigmund Freud

One of the most difficult parts of finding success in life is complacency. I fully admit I suffer from this affliction more often than I care to acknowledge. It can be nice to relax and enjoy the rewards you have been striving for. The challenge is that nothing lasts forever. Even the best circumstances need tending to endure very long.

In order to remain focused on positive growth, you should constantly be reflecting on all the factors and choices that brought you to your current place in life. In many ways this results in circling back around and redoing the first three sections of this book. Hopefully, this becomes easier as you are starting from a more positive position the second time around. However, it is also inevitable that you change over time. The person you believed yourself to be three years ago no longer exists. The events, even positive ones, have shaped you into a new person. It is critical to reflect, review, and refine your sense of self. The following are just a few examples of things you can try to keep your perspective fresh and ever growing.

Do you remember the time tracker from many pages back? You know, the one you likely spent a good amount of time cursing me for making you do. Well, its back.

During the first stages of really growing and expanding we are normally hyper focused and understand the need to maximize time. As we grow into our success it becomes natural to allow other less important time wasters to creep in. It is very likely we don't even realize it as it happens.

Slowly over time the creep becomes a full slide. Where we once remained laser focused on priorities, we now accept some give. This can result in a shift over time that pushes us farther and farther away from the ideal life we thought to live. In order to combat this, we must reevaluate the time log every now and again.

We need to take a serious look at where our time is going and decide if it remains in balance with our desired life. This exercise can in some ways be more difficult the second time around. Initially we are driven to increase the time devoted to pursuing the perfect life. The singular focus gives us purpose and makes accounting for time straight forward. The shift to a more balanced life, however, can cause the need to reexamine exactly what our balanced life is meant to be.

My suggestion is to ask yourself the simple question of whether the items reflected in your time log are worthy of your efforts. Perhaps they represent a new desire. Perhaps your time is spent drastically differently than when you first began the journey. This is all fine, as long as you are aware and accept it as worthy of your effort.

* * *

Along with redoing your time tracker, it is time to reflect and refine your Convergence Point. It may well be the case that these specific pieces of who you are never change. In fact, there is a good argument if they are done correctly the first time they won't change. The core essence of who you are as a person is unlikely to change throughout life. In some cases, there may be major life events that alter your way of thinking. In any case, it is important to know these answers in your heart.

Your life is and will always be directed by what you value. Taking the time to reflect on what inspires you, what motivates you, and what you excel at will ensure your life stays centered around the convergence of these three things.

* * *

My final piece of advice when you begin reflecting is to remember clearly all the times you said no to people in order to focus on the critical tasks before you. I say this because I believe you should say "no" more often moving forward. During your rise it was easier to say no. You were so focused on the path you laid out for yourself you were able to deflect the requests that varied from it. Now, however, you are in the more relaxed phase. This naturally leads to other people believing they can begin directing your time for you.

The whole driver behind this book was to live the life you choose with direction coming from inside. My guess is you went on this journey to gain control over your decisions, your time, and your life. There is no reason to backslide now. Your success will naturally bring with it people asking for assistance and advice. This can quickly turn into demands on your time that are outside of your chosen path. You must become an expert at saying no. Keep in mind "No" is a complete sentence. You don't owe explanations of why you choose to follow your path to anyone. I have made it clear I believe you should find a solid way to give back and help others rise. However, like everything else it must be done on your terms.

Chapter 20
NEXT?

"Success is not final, failure is not fatal: it is the courage to continue that counts."
-Winston Churchill

The winding path of this life never truly ends, until it does. No matter your point in life there is plenty yet to do. Your focus should remain on the next great adventure. You will move forward whether you choose to or not. The world will spin tomorrow, and the sun will rise. You can spend time reflecting on all the past glory you have attained. Yet, the world will keep spinning. Therefore, my final question to you is simple.

What's NEXT?

If you are struggling to come up with an answer to this question, I have a great suggestion. Go back to page 1 of this book and start over. The future holds something you and you alone were meant to achieve. Find it. You owe it to yourself and the world to live an **AUTHENTIC** life.

I want to thank you one last time for allowing me to narrate this journey for you. If you gain even one piece of insight into a better future path for yourself, I will consider it a win. It has been an honor, and I welcome you to the Flame Keepers.

-Jason

Work Pages

Time Log: 30 Minute Blocks
What are you DOING?

Day 1

Time by Category:

Sleep   _____
Work   _____
Entertainment _____
Other (name it) _____
Other   _____
Other   _____
Other   _____
Other   _____

Day 2

Time by Category:

Sleep   _____
Work   _____
Entertainment _____
Other (name it) _____
Other   _____
Other   _____
Other   _____
Other   _____

Day 3

Time by Category:

Sleep   _____
Work   _____
Entertainment _____
Other (name it) _____
Other   _____
Other   _____
Other   _____
Other   _____

Day 4

Time by Category:

Sleep   _____
Work   _____
Entertainment _____
Other (name it) _____
Other   _____
Other   _____
Other   _____
Other   _____

Day 5

Time by Category:

Sleep _____
Work _____
Entertainment _____
Other (name it) _____
Other _____
Other _____
Other _____
Other _____

Day 6

Time by Category:

Sleep _____
Work _____
Entertainment _____
Other (name it) _____
Other _____
Other _____
Other _____
Other _____

Day 7

Time by Category:

Sleep   _____
Work   _____
Entertainment _____
Other (name it) _____
Other   _____
Other   _____
Other   _____
Other   _____

Time Log Grand Totals

Time by Category:

Sleep   _____
Work   _____
Entertainment _____
Other (name it) _____
Other   _____
Other   _____
Other   _____
Other   _____

Notes to Yourself:

1 thing I should spend more time on?

_____

1 thing I should spend less time on?

_____

Random thoughts:

_____

_____

_____

Habit Breakdown

Dumb Habit 1 (you identified these in chapter 13)

Cue_____

Craving_____

Response_____

Reward_____

Which step will you specifically target to change or break the habit (and how)?

_____

_____

Dumb Habit 2 (you identified these in chapter 13)

Cue_____

Craving_____

Response_____

Reward_____

Which step will you specifically target to change or break the habit (and how)?

_____

_____

Dumb Habit 3 (you identified these in chapter 13)

Cue_____

Craving_____

Response_____

Reward_____

Which step will you specifically target to change or break
the habit (and how)?

_____

_____

Smart Habit 1 (time for some new ones)

Habit_____

Cue_____

Craving_____

Response_____

Reward_____

Smart Habit 2 (time for some new ones)

Habit_____

Cue_____

Craving_____

Response_____

Reward_____

Smart Habit 3 (time for some new ones)

Habit_____

Cue_____

Craving_____

Response_____

Reward_____

Made in the USA
Monee, IL
05 March 2020

22761498R00095